POU HAKANONONGA

A Statue from Easter Island

Nicolas Cauwe

2024

PLUS Masterpieces

ROYAL MUSEUMS
OF ART AND HISTORY

To my wife, Dominique Coupé, and my colleagues,
Dirk Huyge and Johnny De Meulemeester,
all three of whom died far too soon.

―――

Our foursome was the mainstay of the research by
the Royal Museums of Art and History on Easter Island.

CONTENT

The arrival of a stone giant in Brussels   7
Easter Island and the Indus Valley   7
The participants of the Franco-Belgian expedition   9
Brussels on Easter Island time   16

The gift of a *moai*?   21
Chilean procrastination   21
The Rapa Nui restore the transport
of a statue   22
Pascuan friendships of   25
the Franco-Belgian mission

The statue's name   35
Nicknames for the *moai*   35
The god of tuna fishermen   37
Traditions of yesterday and today   40
Two names for one *moai*   45

In search of the history
of Pou Hakanononga   51
Pierre Loti on Easter Island   52
Exploration of Ahu o Rongo   56
Life expectancy of the *ahu-moai*   60
The *moai* and the whale   64
Ceremonies around the *ahu*   66

An archaic statue — 71
- Pou Hakanononga and Tukuturi — 71
- A Polynesian statue — 76
- Stories of ears — 78
- Of flesh and bone — 80
- The fishhooks of Pou Hakanononga — 86
- The "mystery" of the Rapa Nui statues — 90

The country (almost) without *moai* — 93

- Notes — 97
- References — 101
- Index of Polynesian terms used in the text — 105
- Illustration credits — 109

THE ARRIVAL OF A STONE GIANT IN BRUSSELS

Easter Island and the Indus Valley

On Monday, 13 May 1935, at about 5:00 pm, after a journey around the world of nearly eight months, the *Mercator*, the Belgian merchant-navy training ship, entered Brussels at the Van Praet Bridge, its last stop before returning to its home port of Antwerp (fig. 1). According to press reports of the time, many onlookers lined the banks of the canal from Vilvoorde, while amateur sailors, kayaks and other canoes volunteered to escort the *Mercator*,[1] while "the dense and emotional crowd was kept at bay by a police cordon".[2] The ship's return was always an event, but this time there was an added edge to the usual festivities, since the *Mercator* was bringing a most wonderful shipment back to Belgium, an authentic Easter Island statue!

Fig. 1

Arrival of the *Mercator* at the Brussels Yacht Club, upstream of the Van Praet Bridge, on the evening of Monday, 13 May 1935 (*La Libre Belgique*, 15 May 1935).

Built in the Scottish shipyards in 1931, this 78 m barquentine (or schooner barque), which is now a museum in the port of Ostend, embarked on its maiden voyage to train officer candidates in 1932. During its seventh voyage, from October 1934 to May 1935, it was asked

Fig. 2

Comparison between the signs of the Indus civilisation, 3rd millennium BCE (on the left in each column) and those of the Easter Island tablets, 15th – 18th centuries CE (on the right in each column). This comparison, established by Guillaume de Hevesy, takes neither geographical spaces nor temporalities into account, although it is the result of a selection, keeping the signs that have equivalents on both sides, and disregarding all those, more numerous, that do not have a symmetrical counterpart (according to de Hevesy 1932).

to anchor off Easter Island and pick up the members of a scientific expedition, subsequently called the "Franco-Belgian mission to Easter Island".

The craziest theories are sometimes the starting point for some of the most serious scientific works. The Franco-Belgian mission of 1934-1935 stems from just such an opposition. In 1932, an amateur Hungarian linguist, Vilmos Hevesy, who preferred to be known in France by the less exotic and more stylish name of Guillaume de Hevesy, proposed an audacious comparison between the Easter Island "writing" (the famous wooden tablets, covered with signs called *kohau rongorongo**) and the "hieroglyphs" discovered in the Indus Valley in the 1920s, on the sites of Mohenjo-Daro and Harappa (fig. 2).[3] Today, the favourable response that part of the scientific community gave to Guillaume de Hevesy's theory is surprising, since it defied all chronological, geographical and cultural obstacles: more than 20,000 km separate the Indus Valley and Easter Island, and while the Mohenjo-Daro civilisation dates back to the 3rd millennium BCE, that of Easter Island dates to the 1st and 2nd millennia CE. Had his theory been correct, we could link all civilisations together, which some people are still quick to do, wanting the Mesopotamians,

---

* There is an index of terms in Polynesian languages at the end of the volume.

Egyptians and other Phoenicians to be the origin of all the "mysteries" of distant lands.

The participants of the Franco-Belgian expedition

Be that as it may, Paul Rivet (1876-1958), then director of the Musée du Trocadéro (the future Musée de l'Homme in Paris) and a fervent diffusionist, was drawn to Guillaume de Hevesy's work. Would the "mysteries" of Easter Island finally be unlocked? He decided to mount an expedition to Rapa Nui (the Polynesian name for Easter Island) in the hope of finding other writing tablets to determine their origin and meaning. He appointed Louis-Charles Watelin (1874-1934) to lead the expedition. An experienced archaeologist and a specialist in Mesopotamia, where he had directed many excavations, Watelin was familiar with the discoveries made at Mohenjo-Daro. However, before the mission departed on the *Rigault de Genouilly*, a French Navy aviso, Paul Rivet wanted to know a little more about the Easter Island writing tablets. A quick investigation taught him that several of them were kept at Braine-le-Comte, in a convent for the Congregation of the Sacred Hearts of Jesus and Mary (also known as the Congregation of Picpus, after the name of the street where its main headquarters were located in Paris), a religious order that had been responsible for a large part of the evangelisation of Eastern Polynesia, including Rapa Nui. In their luggage, the good fathers had brought back sculptures and tablets from Easter Island (fig. 3). Rivet looked for a correspondent in Belgium to go to Braine-le-Comte and met a certain Henri Lavachery.

For a long time, Henri Lavachery (1885-1972), a classical philologist, worked only in the industrial world, but his passions lay elsewhere. He was one of the founders of the Société des Américanistes de Belgique, while he was in charge of the American section of the Royal Museums of Art and History on a voluntary basis. He very quickly became fascinated with all the "primitive" arts. On meeting Rivet, Lavachery became enthusiastic about the idea of an expedition and managed to convince the Frenchman to let him take part in the adventure. Rivet made it a condition that Lavachery would have to finance his trip himself.

Fig. 3

Aruku tablet. This Easter Island tablet, formerly kept at Braine-le-Comte in Belgium, is now deposited in the Archives of the Congregation of the Sacred Hearts of Jesus and Mary in Rome (photo of a cast kept at the Royal Museums of Art and History, inv. ET.36.8.2).

There were many obstacles and Lavachery could not immediately find the resources for his trip. Consequently, Paul Rivet looked for a replacement and suggested to one of his former students, the Swiss Alfred Métraux (1902-1963), that he should become part of the team. Métraux had the advantage of already having a rich scientific career despite his youth (he was barely thirty when he was invited to go to Rapa Nui), along with a perfect command of Spanish, following a childhood and schooling in Argentina. Although considerably irritated by Guillaume de Hevesy's theories, Métraux was attracted by the idea of a boat trip along the African coast, and Rivet promised him a position in Paris or a mission in Africa upon his return, which he never received. However, Métraux was not fooled by the motivations of Rivet and Watelin: "Indifferent to the modern Pascuans and the traditions which may still survive on the island, they were already seeing the walls of Sumerian cities appearing beneath their pickaxes. The affinities between Easter Island and Mesopotamia were clear in advance. The trenches that would be dug at the foot of the volcanoes would reveal a lost world. As for me, I was attracted by those few Polynesians who had survived the disaster and who continued to speak their ancient language and tell their legends at the foot of the statues. I was not unaware of their decline, their forgetfulness of the customs and religion of their ancestors, but I hoped, against hope, that in the few practices that had survived and in the tales that I wanted to collect in the original language, I could find a faint whisper of ages past and look at the issue on a new basis."[4]

On 2 March 1934, Lavachery had to watch on annoyed as the *Rigault de Genouilly* departed from the port of Lorient for a journey along the African coast, before reaching Chile and Peru and finally French Polynesia, via Easter Island. But this delay of several months gave him hope. Through the intervention of Adolphe Stoclet, the famous Brussels banker, he finally obtained the financing he needed from the Belgian Ministry of Public Instruction. He also succeeded in getting the Navy to send the *Mercator* to look for the expedition a few months later. Lavachery left Antwerp on 2 June 1934 and caught up with the French expedition in Lima. In the meantime, Louis-Charles Watelin had died of pneumonia contracted during the stopover in Patagonia (Chile). Alfred Métraux therefore found himself as Mission Director, accompanied only by Henri Lavachery, for whom he was supposed to have been the replacement! (fig. 4) The two men finally arrived on Easter Island on 28 July 1934 and ended up leaving on 2 January 1935. Five months to understand Easter Island!

Everything was against Henri Lavachery and Alfred Métraux. The 49-year-old Belgian had little scientific background. The Swiss, 17 years his junior, had international training in ethnography, strong field experience and had written numerous publications. The former was an enthusiast who liked the good things in life, while the latter was there against his will and was neurasthenic by nature. However, a real friendship was born from this expedition, and while Métraux tempered his companion's enthusiasm for the "mysteries", Lavachery facilitated the work through the quality of his relationships with the Islanders. The younger man taught scientific skills to the elder, who took no offence and was the happy companion in a quest which consequently took a turn and no longer had any connection with the extravagant ideas that had prevailed during its organisation. For five months, Métraux applied an unequalled precision to his investigation work and Lavachery very quickly understood that any hopes that major excavations would reveal the vestiges of a "lost civilisation" were simply pipe dreams. However, the Belgian found a field in which he could express himself brilliantly,

that of the engraved rocks (rock art) that were scattered across Easter Island and to which no one had yet paid any sustained attention (fig. 5).

Alfred Métraux was therefore the last person to produce a real ethnographic survey of Easter Island,[5] before the disappearance of the last witnesses to cultural life before evangelisation, which had begun in 1864. While Henri Lavachery revealed a hitherto unknown aspect of Easter Island, that of art engraved on rock walls,[6] and the revival of wood carving on Easter Island in the early twentieth century. Upon their return, both published a short work intended for the general public, where – each in their own way – they recounted the events of their stay in Rapa Nui and the research that they carried out there.[7] Of all their contributions, the best remembered will be the definitive demonstration of the Pascuans' inclusion in the Polynesian world, the cultural uniqueness that has spanned the history of this island and the absence of ancient settlements with fantastic intellectual and technological possibilities.

Fig. 4

Henri Lavachery (left) and Alfred Métraux (right) on the *Rigault de Genouilly* in July 1934, a few days before their arrival on Easter Island.

Fig. 5

Henri Lavachery about to leave on an expedition to Easter Island, 1934.

Alfred Métraux enjoyed a brilliant career, notably in Honolulu as a Researcher at the Bernice Pauahi Bishop Museum. He also taught at the universities of Berkeley and Yale, was Head of Research at the United Nations Department of Economic and Social Affairs, and a Researcher at the Smithsonian Institution in Washington, DC, before returning to Paris to take up a post as Director of Studies at the École Pratique des Hautes Études and to work for UNESCO. A global citizen, he acquired both French and American nationalities during his career. Following his retirement, he sadly committed suicide on 11 April 1963 at the age of 61. In a publication written by the essayist Étienne Barilier, Switzerland recently paid tribute to this great ethnologist so long ignored in his native country.[8] This biography, which happily combines the most remarkable traits of the man and the scientist, does justice to Métraux, who is often described as cold and distant.

Henri Lavachery achieved recognition of his talents in Belgium. He would have the daunting task of managing the Royal

Loading of Pou Hakanononga's statue on the *Mercator*, January 1935

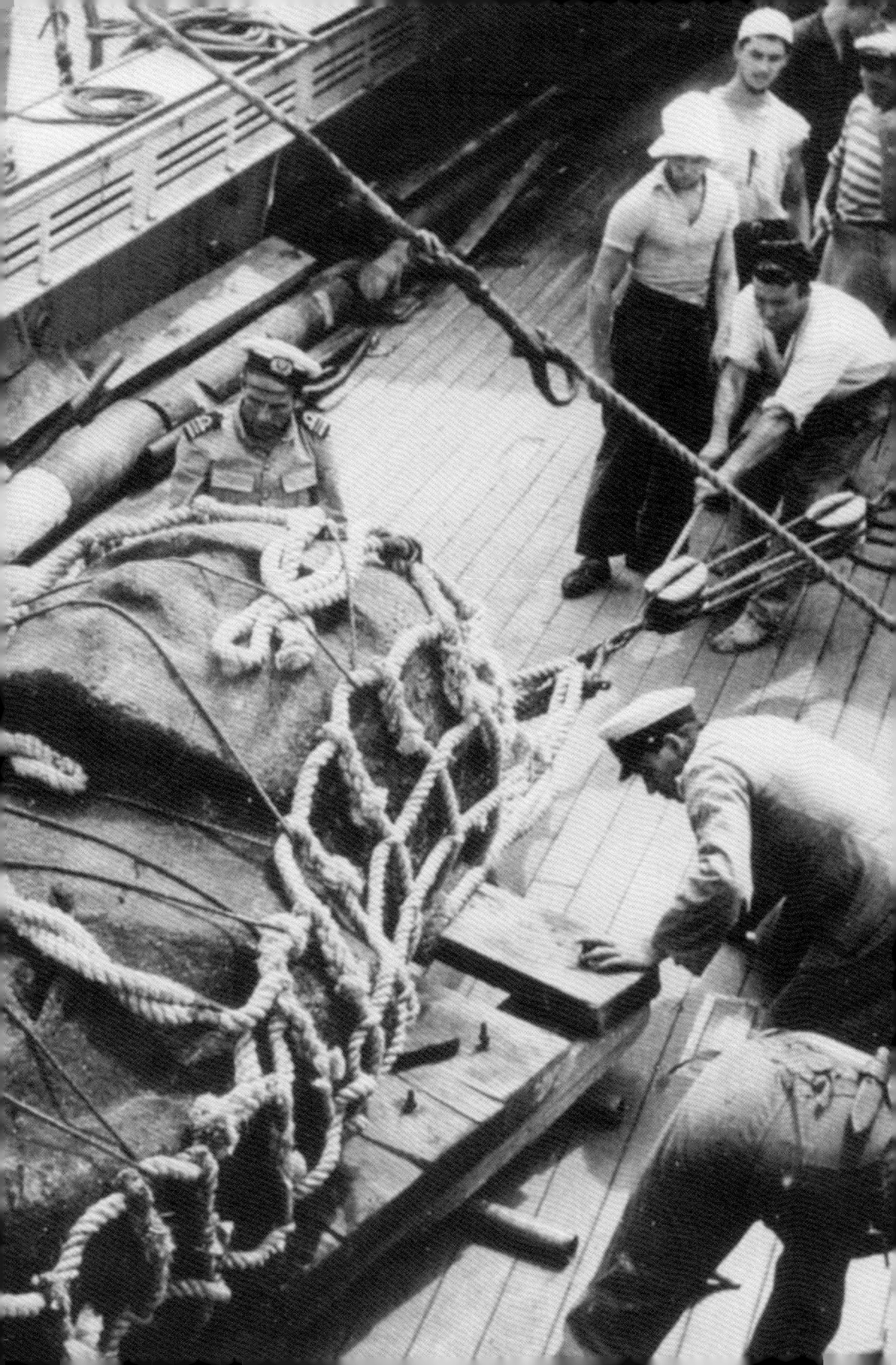

Museums of Art and History during the Second World War (from 1942), before sourcing courses at the Université Libre de Bruxelles and later becoming Permanent Secretary of the Fine Arts section of the Royal Academy of Belgium. He died in 1972 at the age of 87. In 2002, his grandson Thomas made a film about his Pascuan saga (*L'Homme de Pâques*, a Triangle 7, RTBF and WIP co-production) and wrote an endearing book describing the duality and friendship that marked the relationship between Alfred Métraux and his grandfather.[9] In more scientific terms, but with the most captivating writing, Christine Laurière produced a well-documented overview a few years ago of this 1934-1935 expedition – a truly historic event that has remained in the memory, as much for the Rapa Nui as the scientific world.[10]

Brussels on Easter Island time

Let's go back to Easter Island. The work of Alfred Métraux and Henri Lavachery concluded with the Chilean government's gift of a statue for Belgium and the head of another for France. The arrival of these "trophies" in Europe made a strong impression, especially the statue destined for Belgium. Henri Lavachery even had his caricature on the cover of the weekly newspaper *Pourquoi Pas?*[11] (fig. 6), and was given a private audience with King Leopold III, who had ascended the throne a year earlier. The most was quickly made of the opportunity and on Tuesday, 28 May 1935, just fifteen days after the arrival of the *Mercator* in Brussels, ministers, intellectuals, artists, and the general public rushed to the Royal Museums of Art and History to admire the wonders brought back from Rapa Nui. Among the many people welcomed by Jean Capart, Chief Curator of the Museums, were His Excellency Mr Jorge Valdès-Mendeville, Ambassador of Chile (or Minister of Chile, as he was called at the time), and Mr François Bovesse, Minister of Public Instruction, who reminded the audience that "material concerns do not prevent the government from taking an interest in essential things, in art, science and thought". He ended his speech by thanking the Chilean government, which "through its generous gesture had earned the gratitude of the scientific world".[12]

Fig. 6

Cover van *Pourquoi Pas?* van vrijdag 31 mei 1935.

For a few days, Brussels lived on Easter Island time. The excitement obviously petered out and the statue was quickly forgotten in its exhibition room at the Cinquantenaire Museum (fig. 7), admired only by those interested in museums, or by a few scholars with more professional interests. However, there are hardly any museums that can rely on such testimony. The British Museum boasts two giants, one named Hoa Hakananani'a, the other Moai Hava, removed in 1868 by

HMS *Topaz*, a British navy ship. They were presented by the Lord of the Admiralty (Minister of the Navy) to Queen Victoria in 1869, who immediately gifted them to the British Museum. Paris has two statue heads on display, the first at the Quai Branly-Jacques Chirac Museum, which was put aboard *La Flore* in 1872, and the second, the one which arrived on the *Mercator* in 1935, is exhibited at the Louvre. That's it for Europe! And there's not much more elsewhere. The Smithsonian Museum in Washington has a small two-metre-high statue, another that is not much larger, but has a red scoria headdress, and the head of a third, all of which were taken by the *USS Mohican* in 1887. In 1928, the Otago Museum in Dunedin, New Zealand, purchased a small *moai* (anthropomorphic figure in the Rapanui language) from the Brander family, who had a farm on Rapa Nui in the 1870s. It is clearly a fairly late creation made in the nineteenth century and intended for passing sailors. The Museum of Natural History in Santiago de Chile has just returned (February 2022) to Easter Island the statue it had owned since 1878. There are only six complete *moai* outside of Rapa Nui: two in London (1869), two in Washington (1887), one in New Zealand (1928), and the sixth... in Brussels (1935).

Fig. 7

Pou Hakanononga, as it was installed in 1936 in the permanent rooms of the Royal Museums of Art and History.

THE GIFT OF A *MOAI*?

Chilean procrastination

The Brussels statue is the only one known to have been given with the Rapa Nui's consent. But is it really a gift? The island was annexed by Chile in 1888 and so the 1934-1935 Franco-Belgian mission had to have the permission of the Chilean authorities. Following the instructions received from Santiago, this approval was issued orally by Ernan Cornejo Alemparte, Civil Governor of the island (the *subdelegado* of the Chilean government) to mark the arrival of the *Mercator* in December 1934. He authorised the Belgian ship to take the *moai* head that Alfred Métraux had chosen for France and the statue selected for Belgium by Henri Lavachery and Remi Van de Sande, Commander of the *Mercator*.[13] As early as January 1935, however, there were articles in the Chilean press reporting a violent theft. Alfred Métraux gave the following brief account: "But when news of the statue's removal reached Chile, it was another thing. People who would have been particularly indifferent to the annihilation of Easter Island and its inhabitants shed tears over the abducted statue. We had deprived Chile of its most beautiful pride and joy; the country was impoverished by the base greed of foreigners. They gave a sensationalised description of our landing, bayonets fixed, the Governor tied up, the natives brutally forced to give up the cherished gods of their ancestors."[14]

In a letter dated 19 August 1935, addressed to Paul Van Zeeland, Minister for Foreign Affairs of the Belgian government, Maxime Gérard, the Belgian ambassador to

Chile, commented on this totally unfounded dispute.[15] The argument had allegedly been started by the Rector of the State University of Chile and by Mons. Rafael Edwards, Bishop of Santiago, who had Easter Island in his diocese and who had been trying to have the rights of its inhabitants recognised by the Chilean authorities since 1917. Maxime Gérard insisted, however, that the statue's removal by the Franco-Belgian mission was the responsibility of the Chilean subdelegado in Rapa Nui. The incident finally made the Chilean government aware of the need to arrange protection for the heritage of Easter Island, which had until then been totally ignored by the administration in charge of national property. The Franco-Belgian mission was therefore indirectly responsible for Chile's awareness of the importance of the archaeological remains on Easter Island. Nevertheless, on Friday, 18 December 1936, at the opening of the Mercator Room in the Royal Museums of Art and History, the Chilean ambassador, Jorge Valdès-Mendeville, definitively confirmed that the collections gathered on Easter Island were being gifted to Belgium, including the famous statue. He was thanked on behalf of the Belgian government by the newly appointed Minister of Public Education, Mr Julius Hoste.[16] So much for the official version.

The Rapa Nui restore the transport of a statue

But what about the indigenous population, which had no administrative or legal representation at the time? The account by Mr Pasquier, the Wireless Operator on board the *Mercator*, is very interesting in this regard. He was asked for his comments by the newspaper *Le Soir*, on the arrival of the *Mercator* in Brussels in May 1935: – "Well, at first, we believed that the Easter Island population would have shown us some hostility when they saw that we were trying to take away one of their ancient deities. But, on the contrary, as soon as they saw us hauling on the ropes which we had looped around the blocks of stone to drag them to the beach, all of them, men, women, children, got started to work alongside us. I can assure you that we were surprised. So, we pulled our load into the water. Then we tied the ropes to a rowing boat and swam to the boat. There we hooked the hoists to the ropes and started

Fig. 8

One of the Pascuan divers who courageously tried to recover the statue that had fallen to a depth of 20 m, after a hoist on the *Mercator* broke.

to haul. But disaster struck during the first loading: the ropes broke, and the statue fell to the seabed. As it was several metres deep at that point, none of us could manage to repair the damage by diving. We were very embarrassed." – "So, what did you do?" – "It was the natives who saved us. These people dive in an extraordinary way, staying under for three minutes working at a depth of several metres (fig. 8). We wondered how they could withstand such pressure."[17]

Alfred Métraux gave us a rather similar, but more detailed report: "We nearly had some trouble with the natives who, suddenly seized with a great local patriotism, spoke of making money from the insult inflicted on their national treasure. These fanatics of the past were the first to lend us their support, when they discovered that they could be given a few

Fig. 9

December 1934. Sailors from the *Mercator* and Easter Islanders all help to transport the statue that would be taken to Brussels.

small gifts. Most of the natives sensibly reasoned: "We have so many statues that one more or less doesn't make much difference. We ourselves destroy them and sell the pieces to the sailors on the *Baquedano*" [the *General Baquedano*, a Chilean training ship which made about twenty voyages to Rapa Nui]. [...] This is a faithful account of these events as they happened in the real world. The *Mercator* was facing a daunting task. The statue weighed about 4 to 5 tonnes. We didn't have a raft and we were worried about whether the rowing boat would hold the weight. First, the statue had to be taken out of its hole, which was done using a hoist. We only managed to raise it a few centimetres, but that was enough to put it in a net and then put it on a sledge. The second part of the operation allowed us to relive the island's legendary past for a few hours. It involved hauling the statue to the shore. The Commander had two ropes attached to it and fifty sailors set to work. Muscles tensed, faces became flushed, but the statue did not move. Suddenly, one Pascuan, then two, then a whole crowd grabbed the ropes. We pulled a third time; the statue shook and moved forward a few centimetres. This time, the women came running, then the young mothers with their babies on one hip and finally some old grandmothers with no illusions about the usefulness of their help (fig. 9). Soon everyone was repeating the chant for pulling. *Iaho, hoooohoppp!* The statue was reluctant again, then suddenly started and slid onto the rollers placed under the sledge's runners."[18]

As for Henri Lavachery, he primarily described the people's joy as the giant was transported: "Long ropes were attached to the cart [sledge]. More than a hundred Pascuans, men, women and children, twenty cadets, officers and ourselves were all pulling on these ropes. Hanga One One [the name Lavachery gave to the statue] slid on the grass amidst shouts of joy from the people. A rope broke. Around fifty of us falling on the ground caused more delight. At the end of the day, the sledge carrying the statue reached the beach. The volunteer haulers snacked on cookies and smoked the cigarettes distributed by the commander. Comments flew around in the midst of growing enthusiasm."[19]

Pascuan friendships of the Franco-Belgian mission

These testimonies are largely confirmed by the film that was made on this occasion. The shots were taken by a young, 21-year-old Dutch filmmaker John Fernhout (1913-1987, son of the painter Charley Toorop, herself daughter of the painter Jan Toorop), who was responsible for following the voyage of the *Mercator*. The material gathered by Fernhout was then sent to Henri Storck (1907-1999), who edited and produced a small 35 mm film entitled *Easter Island* (1935). In this short film (26 mins), we can clearly see the entire island population helping the sailors to pull the statue to the shore in a festive atmosphere. There is no refusal from the islanders with regard to Belgium taking this trophy to Brussels.

It must be said that in five months of working on the island, Alfred Métraux and Henri Lavachery had established strong bonds of friendship and respect. Their testimonies when they left Rapa Nui and boarded the Belgian ship speak for themselves. Henri Lavachery told us the following story:

"In the shade, we kiss some wet cheeks. Little Ana is handed to me. She puts her arms around my neck; we hug Tepano close to our hearts. [...] 'Adios Enlique, Adios Alfredo.' Familiar voices follow us, moving away. An indistinct group on the jetty melts into the night. Would we ever return to Easter Island?"[20] Alfred Métraux added: "Two days later, we were leaving. Victoria was very emotional, and tears were streaming down her cheeks. To console her I said, 'I'll come back...' She shook her head and in a disillusioned voice murmured, 'You don't come back to Easter Island. When you leave here, it's as if you died.' Lavachery was deeply moved, and I was haunted by my friend's words. I looked at things and people as if I was in agony. The good Tepano drew on his pipe a little nervously and said: 'Alfredo, you have all the tales of the island.' Little Mata wanted to seem indifferent, but her eyes were wet; Maria Ika waved her hand in a monotonous movement, and the elderly Pons looked like a ghost of the past. They were all there, those people with whom we had lived as closely with as if we had been on the same boat. Isn't Easter Island a motionless ship in the middle of the seas?"[21]

Alfred Métraux tells us another fact: "The day after [loading the statue onto the *Mercator*], in the village of Hanga Roa, the old lady Maria Ika approached me and said: 'I composed a song in honour of the statue. Do you want to hear it?' She intoned the following words:
They pulled you from the ahu Orongo by pulling on ropes
O you Pou-Haka-nononga, god of the tuna fishermen.
They pulled you with their ropes
These happy strangers who had landed.
They will take you away.
They will raise you again on a mausoleum
In Belgium where young girls will come to look at you".[22]

All of these testimonies – written, photographed, or filmed – agree on one point: in December 1934, the people of Easter Island were in no way frustrated by the removal of one of their statues. They all took part in its transportation, even in the most difficult moments, notably recovering it from the bottom of the ocean after a hoist on the *Mercator* broke. Of course, there is no written document that officially establishes the Islanders' gift. But they could not produce such a

Fig. 10
Previous page:

The *Mercator* off Easter Island (December 1934).

Fig. 11

Juan Tepano – the principal source of local information for the Franco-Belgian expedition and whose mother was still alive in 1934 – had experienced the times before the island's evangelisation document since they were not listed in a population register and had no passport or financial means. But their friendship for "Enlique" Lavachery and "Alfredo" Métraux is widely demonstrated. In 1999, 64 years later, Nicolás Haoa still remembered the Belgian and the Franco-Swiss visit very well and told the following story: "I was a very young kid at the time. But on the day of departure [of the *Mercator*], Alfredo [Métraux] asked me what souvenir I would like of him. I had been admiring his watch for months and asked him for it. He said no, because he knew what would happen: 'It won't be five minutes', he said, 'before you drop it, and it breaks'. But I insisted, I cried, and finally he gave me his watch. I could still see the boat on the horizon (fig. 10), and I had already dropped the watch, which was lying in a thousand pieces."[23]

The quality of the relationships that Alfred Métraux and Henri Lavachery had with the Rapa Nui is due to several

Fig. 12

Victoria Rapahango with Henri Lavachery, Easter Island 1934.

elements. First of all, their deep empathy for the Polynesians of Easter Island, who lived, at that time, in extreme poverty. Each in their own way – Métraux more reserved, Lavachery more extrovert – they won the confidence of the Rapa Nui and even formed quite a strong friendship with some of them, firstly with Juan Tepano (1867-1947; fig. 11), their main source of information, and with Victoria Rapahango (1895-1979; fig. 12) who worked with Métraux for weeks on the Rapanui-language version of the myths collected by the Swiss man.

Métraux and Lavachery lived with the Rapa Nui for five months, sharing the miserable conditions of their existence. For once, there was no question of foreigners arriving fully equipped and living on the fringes of the population. It is also worth noting the close friendship between Alfred Métraux, Henri Lavachery and Victoria Rapahango, although the intimacy of this friendship is unknown. This young

Fig. 13

From left to right: Henri Lavachery, Alfred Métraux and Israël Dapkin on the *Rigault de Genouilly* in July 1934.

woman of royal lineage exerted a certain fascination on the two explorers. Henri Lavachery even considered bringing Victoria's daughter, Ana, then aged 3, back to Belgium – a child whose biological father was a passing sailor, long since gone. Lavachery, who acted like a grandfather to Ana, would have liked to have given her a European education. At the last minute, on the deck of the *Mercator*, Victoria refused to be separated from her daughter. Although she has never left her island, Ana, now in her nineties, still feels a bit "Belgian".

Finally, the Franco-Belgian mission agreed to the presence of a doctor, Israël Drapkin (fig. 13), who the Chilean authorities insisted upon as the "official supervisor" of the expedition. However, Drapkin firstly actively cared for the island's lepers. All this humanism generated a recognition and respect among the Islanders for these curious visitors who bore little resemblance to previous ones. The Norwegian Thor Heyerdahl,

who also had a deep respect for the Oceanians, had a similar experience in 1955, during his stay on this island at the end of the world.

So no, the Brussels statue was not "officially" gifted by the Rapa Nui! They agreed that it could be taken away out of "friendship" with Henri Lavachery and Alfred Métraux, in recognition of a powerful human experience.

Previous page:

Young girl from Easter Island, 1934

THE STATUE'S NAME

Nicknames for the *moai*

In March 1774, James Cook was the first to record a series of names that the Rapa Nui had given to their statues.[24] The great British navigator noted that these names were often preceded by the prefix *moai* and sometimes followed by the suffix *areekee*. It is now known that the word *moai* refers to any anthropomorphic figure (large stone statues, as well as small wooden figurines), while *ariki* translates as "chief" or "king". In all likelihood, the large *moai* were associated with ancestral *ariki*.

However, from the end of the nineteenth century, the types of names that the Pascuans gave the statues had changed. Métraux was therefore surprised that the names referring to particular characters or deities had almost disappeared, his local guides instead giving him names of a descriptive nature, such as "Twisted neck" or "Tattooed", and even very unappealing ones, such as "Smelly" (fig. 14).[25] A few years earlier, the British woman Katherine Routledge (1866-1935) had identified the same situation.[26] A part of the traditions therefore seems to have been lost since the time of the first contacts. There is little doubt that the designations recorded by Routledge or Métraux are nothing other than recent names, born of the imagination of the islanders who agreed to give the stone giants nicknames that would allow them to be identified and recognised, a practice that is still used to designate passing strangers. The case of the statues taken to London in 1868 is exemplary in this respect. The most famous of these was given the name Hoa Hakananani'a

(the "Wave Tamer")[27] by the Rapa Nui (fig. 15). However, there is some ambiguity as to the meaning of this name, and the British Museum, custodian of this *moai* since 1869, still posts the less complimentary translation of "lost, hidden or stolen friend" on its website.[28] London's other statue has a similarly unflattering name: Moai Hava, which can be translated as "Dirty, repudiated, rejected or lost statue".[29] The Rapa Nui gave the statues these names before these two *moai* were loaded onto HMS *Topaz*. No doubt this is an allusion to statues that they no longer knew and that they rediscovered when the British visited.[30]

Fig. 14

A *moai* called Piro Piro ("Smelly") by the Rapa Nui in 1934. This statue is lying on the external flank of the Rano Raraku volcano, in the southeast of the island (drawing taken from Henri Lavachery's 3rd notebook, compared with a photo *in situ*).

36

Fig. 15

An Easter Monday Group round an Easter Island Statue, drawing published in *The Illustrated London News* of 9 April 1887. The statue depicted here is that of *Hoa Hakananani'a*, "the Wave Tamer" or "the Stolen Friend".

The god of tuna fishermen

In any case, the name Pou Hakanononga that the Pascuans attributed to the statue taken to Brussels in 1934 is of a different order. Literally, a *pou* is a marker for fishermen, while *hakanononga* refers to an area rich in fish. Juan Tepano, the Franco-Belgian mission's main informant, associated the statue with the nearby marine space and explained that it was used to find a *hakanononga* rich in *káhi* (tuna).[31] In a letter that he sent to Henri Lavachery on 17 June 1936, Alfred Métraux reminded him of the testimonies that he had recorded: "I realise that I forgot to give you the details gathered at the beginning of our stay about your statue, Hanga One One [the name that Lavachery had first recorded]. Here they are. On the left, looking at the sea, a large statue (Pouhakanononga). According to tradition, it was a kind of landmark for tuna fishermen. A king would have placed it there to indicate the place where the most fish were caught. It is made of a different rock than the neighbouring statues and does not come from Rano Raraku [the volcano that was used as the quarry for most of the Easter Island statues]. The head is admirable, the back perfectly shaped. The spine is indicated by a sort of channel that leads to a depression at the top of the lower back."[32] (fig. 16)

The Brussels statue would therefore have been a *pou*, which the fishermen would have used to find a *hakanononga* rich in

Fig. 16

Pou Hakanononga. On the left: a profile of the right side of the statue's face. On the right: a detail of its back; the spine is represented by a large hollow line that flares out at the lower back.

tuna. But in Polynesia, for things to be effective they must have *mana*, an intrinsic force. Moreover, we know the propensity of the Pascuans to designate an entity or a spirit by a secondary functional aspect. So, it is not surprising that this Pou Hakanononga was understood as a deity that innately possesses powerful *mana*. In her song, Maria Ika refers to the statue as the god of tuna fishermen.[33]

However, does this name and function date back to the time when the statue was sculpted? The nineteenth century was a catastrophe for the Islanders, wiped out by the diseases brought by European ships, ruined by the abuses of explorers, and decimated by slave raids. In 1877, the French explorer Alphonse Pinart (1852-1911) counted only III natives on the island.[34] So, even before the end of the nineteenth century, any ethnographic approach to the island's history seemed doomed to failure. In 1919, Katherine Routledge implied as much, admitting that the Islanders she had met were unlikely to hold all the keys to their past.[35] So what do the stories told represent? The last shreds of memories faithfully remembered? A reconstruction of the past by survivors cut off from their roots and seeking to recover an identity? None of this can be measured any more. Reason dictates, therefore, that the name of the statue kept in Brussels is considered with some reservations. Archaeological excavations conducted between 2001 and 2003 around the ceremonial platform where Pou Hakanononga was once erected (see below) show that this moai had an eventful history and was buried under ruins for several centuries. This factual information convinces us that the use of this stone giant as a landmark for fishing and its status as a deity are both modern.

Traditions of yesterday and today

The refusal to consider all the accounts recorded since the late nineteenth century as originating directly from tradition will seem indecent to some. Under the guise of combating racism and renouncing the colonial era, indigenous groups are now bestowed with an indestructible oral memory, transmitted unchanged, or only slightly so, over the generations. Some people go so far as to say that local people are the only ones who can understand and reconstruct their history. Unfortunately, these prejudices mean that societies that were still described as savage or primitive in the recent past have remained unchanged for centuries, without the slightest influence of time or external interference. The intention is nothing more than the implicit affirmation of a new "primitivism" marked by stagnation. Historical and ethnological sciences cannot adhere to this "political correctness", not because of moral issues, but for factual reasons: there is no such thing as cultural immobility, whatever the weight of traditions and the obligation to follow them.

In the case of Easter Island, things are even clearer. In 1955, the Norwegian Thor Heyerdahl was the protagonist in an event, the importance of which has perhaps not been fully appreciated. During his archaeological work on Easter Island, many of the workers he hired gave him access to what they called their "secret family caves". These were filled with stone sculptures, many of whose themes were completely foreign to traditional Easter Island art. Thor Heyerdahl immediately perceived a dual problem.[36] Previous researchers, such as Katherine Routledge or Henri Lavachery, had heard of secret caves, but had never had access to them. The Norwegian was therefore intrigued to be the first "initiated" foreigner, but the Rapa Nui told him that he represented a new opportunity for the island and that he "deserved" this disclosure. Thor Heyerdahl's second hesitation was due to the freshness of the sculptures that were presented to him in these caves. However, several clues indicated that these were not just a few quickly made trinkets designed to mislead the explorer for benefit: no financial transaction was required; the impressive number of these objects could not be the result of last-minute work; and there were certain figurative elements that were so strange (skulls, the Virgin Mary, feet, rabbits, cats, etc.) they were not at all suitable for deception, since forgers would instead be looking to imitate tradition in the hope of deceiving. Moreover, Heyerdahl's guides made no secret of the modernity of what they were showing him, speaking of works made by themselves, their wives, parents, or grandparents. Such innocence does not bode well for deception.[37] Thor Heyerdahl had therefore found a popular art that was still current in the 1950s and which remained hidden, apparently for religious reasons, the Pascuans feeling that it

Next page:

Arrival of the statue of Pou Hakanononga to the Royal Museums of Art and History, May 1935

TRANSPORT
CHARELS·F·DIE·G

would not necessarily be appreciated by the Catholic priests, especially since many superstitions were attached to all such figurines amassed in the family caves. The story of these secret caves does not seem very serious, but it could be part of a more fundamental movement of beliefs recreated at the end of the nineteenth century, following the near disappearance of the Rapa Nui as a result of abuses following the encounter with the outside world.

It was only after these tragedies that the first scientific investigations began, although in the testimonies it was impossible to disentangle the traditional elements from the new beliefs developed by the survivors. It seems that all this reconstruction work was established on more popular rather than scholarly bases, with mixtures of ancient beliefs, anachronisms, and data inherent to the new times offering us an original syncretism (fig. 17). It is even probable that the first scientific studies also fed the "tradition". Thus, Henri Lavachery related the following story: "In the afternoon he [Métraux] worked with Tepano who dictated the tales relating to our walk from Hanga Roa to the camp. Métraux, long trained to work with natives through his studies on the Chaco Indians, literally squeezed his guide like a lemon. Tepano was not used to such a

Fig. 17

Basalt figurine (25 cm long), Easter Island, twentieth century. In 1955, the Norwegian Thor Heyerdahl was confronted with these kinds of creations which were presented to him in the "secret family caves". This type of sculpture, quite different in style and theme from traditional productions, was undoubtedly part of the Rapa Nui resilience movement from the end of the nineteenth century (coll. RMAH, inv. ET.85.2.2).

system with Brown,[38] and he tired of answering. He then used a method that is crushing for an ethnographer, who believes he is collecting virgin material: 'You'll find all this in Catarina's book' (Mrs Routledge). But it was more often Brown's book that was mentioned. Nothing could be more discouraging for someone [Métraux] who, naturally inclined to pessimism, sees all his apprehensions confirmed. 'I've always said, and I wrote it down before I left, Easter Island is just an old bone with nothing left to gnaw on.'"[39]

All these syncretisms and interactions are key elements in understanding the current cultural specificity of the Rapa Nui. The gap between the historical facts reconstructed by science and the stories always told is only a mistake for those who do not want to understand its context, that of a society which, like all others, was and is dynamic, but one that also had to completely rebuild itself after the cruel interference of the outside world.

Two names for one *moai*

This context is the final proof that the statue's given name is a recent one. There was some ambiguity over its proper title in 1934. It was called Pou Hakanononga by Juan Tepano and Maria Ika,[40] but Henri Lavachery also recorded the name Moai Hanga One One.[41] *Hanga* translates as "bay" and *one* as "sand", so *hanga one one* is the "[very] sandy bay", which is a local name. But in Rapa Nui, toponyms are often used indiscriminately to name a sector of the island and the monument(s) that are found there (fig. 18). It is therefore hardly surprising that "Hanga One One" might designate both a bay and the statue that stood there. Moai Hanga One One could thus be translated as "the statue that stands near the sandy bay". For the record, Jean-François de Lapérouse, who was sent to the South Seas by Louis XVI and who stopped over at Rapa Nui in 1786, left a short commentary on this place: "This bay is easy to recognise; after passing the two rocks at the southern tip of the island, you must follow the land for a mile, and you soon see a small sandy cove, which is the most certain recognition. Landing is easy enough at the foot of one of the statues that I will speak of shortly."[42]

Fig. 18

Ahu Hanga Tetenga. This toponym refers to the platform (*ahu*) built in the bay (*hanga*) of Tetenga. The Rapa Nui often use the names of localities to designate the monuments that are found there.

The statue mentioned here is probably not Pou Hakanononga: at One One Bay, there are several monuments with which *moai* are associated, and Lapérouse refers us to his commentary on all the island's *moai*, rather than the description of one statue in particular.

The Brussels statue therefore has two names, both probably quite recent: one asserts its function (Pou Hakanononga), the other its location (Hanga One One). There is nothing strange here. Isn't Charles de Gaulle airport also known as Roissy airport? In the first months of its exhibition at Parc du Cinquantenaire, the *moai* brought back by the *Mercator* was presented to the public under the name of Hanga One One. Since then, the name Pou Hakanononga has been used, in order to correspond to the last ministry that the Rapa Nui attributed to this statue, rather than to emphasise the place from where it was taken, a characteristic that was of primary interest to the Islanders, not to visitors to the Museum who are not assumed to have any particular knowledge of the toponymy of Easter Island.

Next page:

Statues (*moai*) erected on the slopes of the Raraku volcano, Easter Island 1934.

IN SEARCH OF THE HISTORY OF POU HAKANONONGA

Fig. 19

Rapa Nui posing on 20 January 1951 in front of the *Manutara*, the first plane to reach Easter Island.

At the time of the Franco-Belgian mission in 1934, Hanga Roa, the only village on Easter Island, was just a small town of 500 souls (including 456 Polynesians)[43] with market gardens. The whole was surrounded by a fence that the islanders could not cross without permission. There was a gate to the north, along the western coast, and another to the east, towards the interior, both guarded. In fact, in 1903, Chile had leased Easter Island to a Scottish company that acted as a despotic landlord and prevented all traffic on the island in order to practice extensive sheep farming, leaving just 20 km² surrounded by barbed wire for the 456 Rapa Nui, and 150 km² of freedom for the 36,000 sheep of the Williamson & Balfour company![44]

Sixteen years later, on 20 January 1951, after a flight of just over nineteen hours, a Catalina seaplane bearing the Rapanui name *Manutara* (*Sterna lunata* or grey-backed tern) landed at Mataveri, south of Hanga Roa (fig. 19). This expedition, which left from La Serena in Chile and was led by Captain Roberto Parragué Singer (1913-1995), was the very first flight to reach Rapa Nui. A wind of change was beginning to blow. Two years later, after half a century of almost absolute control, the Williamson & Balfour Company was forced to pack up (following the non-renewal of its lease) and leave its thousands of sheep.[45] The island then came under the authority of the Chilean Navy. It was not until 1963 that the islanders received Chilean citizenship and were allowed to travel around their island again. In 1967, regular flights were introduced, and in 1984, under the dictatorship of Augusto Pinochet, the post of governor became civilian and was given to an indigenous person.[46] In any case, all these events finally restored some pride to the Polynesians and encouraged economic growth, largely based on tourism. The urban fabric of Hanga Roa was affected by this, with the development of public and private infrastructures, facilitating provincial and municipal administrations, schools, a hospital, airport, roads, water and electricity distribution, hotels, restaurants, shops, and individual houses.

Faced with this redeployment and a significant demographic growth (leading to a population of ± 7,000 inhabitants in 2020), the Pascuan archaeologist Sonia Haoa Cardinali asked the Royal Museums of Art and History in 1999 to undertake archaeological excavations on the Ahu o Rongo site, the current name of Ahu Hanga One One, the site from which Henri Lavachery took the statue of Pou Hakanononga. The aim was to save this place threatened by urban sprawl and already wedged between the small fishing harbour in the city centre and the land reserved for the Tapati – the annual festival, which, to the delight of tourists, reaffirms the Rapanui identity with the help of Polynesians from other islands (fig. 20).

Pierre Loti on Easter Island

The bay in front of Ahu o Rongo is one of the most popular anchorages for sailors. It was here that Jakob Roggeveen dropped anchor on Easter Sunday 1722, a circumstance that led him to give the island a name with Christian conotations. In 1774, James Cook chose the same place to protect his ships, the *Resolution* and the *Adventure*, a choice repeated in 1786 by Jean-François Galaup de Lapérouse for La Boussole and *L'Astrolabe*. In addition, among many other ships, *La Flore*, a French military ship, reached Easter Island on 3 January 1872.

This last expedition had an impact on the Ahu o Rongo site. Indeed, Admiral François-Théodore de Lapelin (1812-1888), who commanded *La Flore*, decided to transport a trophy back to France, but the statues of Ahu o Rongo that were close to his mooring seemed too big. He therefore ordered one of them to be cut up and have its head removed. He also

Fig. 20

Aerial view of the Ahu o Rongo site.
1. A recent monument (built after the fourteenth century), from which the head of a statue was removed by *La Flore*, a French ship that passed through Easter Island in 1872 with Julien Viaud (Pierre Loti) on board; 2. Fourteenth-century platform on which the statue of Pou Hakanononga was erected. 3. The fairground, where the Tapati, the annual festival of Rapa Nui culture, is held; 4. A children's playground. This picture was taken in 2001, since when the urban development of Policarpo Toro Street has evolved significantly.

commissioned a young 22-year-old midshipman who had a talent for drawing to record this scene, now considered perfectly iconoclastic, on paper. This young man, who was born Julien Viaud, would later become famous under the pseudonym Pierre Loti (1850-1923). Loti was horrified by the spectacle presented to him by his fellow travellers and recorded the following account: "It was an expedition to the *morai* [an incorrect transcription of marae, a Tahitian word designating a place of worship] of Cook's Bay [Hanga Roa]; the admiral wanted me to go before the statue was taken down, making an exact drawing, intended for the ministry. Great preparations had been made on board and the rowing boat was going to fetch the colossus, with a hundred men, ropes, levers, pliers, and several other kinds of utensils, all under the

Fig. 21

Julien Viaud (Pierre Loti): *The overturned statue – Easter Island, January 1872.* This was, in fact, the turning over of a statue already laying down at Ahu o Rongo by sailors from *La Flore* and the Pascuans, in order to cut off its head and take it to Paris.

direction of Mr Rod… [Rodolphe], a ship's lieutenant who is considered an artist. The boat, heavily loaded, had difficulty getting through the breakers and finally moored in a suitable position. The natives had gathered in crowds on the beach and were shouting loudly; news of the statue's removal had spread, and they had come from all around to witness the operation. Even those who live in the bay of La Pérouse, on the other side of the island, had come; so we saw many new figures. Mr Rod[olphe], who insisted on the staging, decided that his hundred men would go to the morai in an orderly fashion and on foot, with the bugles sounding the march; this unusual noise put the natives in an indescribable state. The scene that took place at the morai surpassed the horror of the most famous massacres in history and the natives, led by example, proved themselves to be vandals as much as we were. After an hour, everything was devastated, the statues broken, toppled, and it is not yet known which one will have the honour of having its head cut off, to go and appear in the Louvre between the Egyptian divinities and the winged bulls of Assyria. The savages combined their awful work with dances and cries that had nothing human about them. But, standing aside, an old chief, his head bristling with black feathers, contemplated these destructions with sadness and played the role of Mr Couture's Romans.[47] He alone had undoubtedly

Fig. 22

Julien Viaud (Pierre Loti): *Indigenous Ceremony* (January 1872). Imaginary reconstruction of a ceremony in front of a platform with statues. Julien Viaud never claimed that he was drawing a scene he had witnessed. On the contrary, in his notes, he clearly mentions his imagination allowing him to recreate a ceremony at the time of the splendour of the monuments of Rapa Nui.

still respected these sacred things... The chosen statue was lying face down on the ground; it yielded to the efforts of the levers, turned on itself and fell abruptly on its back, without however crushing anyone. Its fall was the signal for a general dance; the savages jumped like madmen, on the face and on the belly, and gambolled until they were out of breath... My drawing is powerless to render the fantastic aspect that the craters then had, with their sharp contrasts of shadow and light, standing out against the black sky; neither does it render these cries, this frenzy. These long dead of primitive races, for the centuries that they had been asleep under their morai, had never heard such a noise, except however that which their statues must have made, when they fell from old age, heavily and one by one, with their noses to the ground..."[48] (fig. 21)

In Europe, an engraving by Janet-Lange (1818-1872, whose real name was Ange-Louis Janet)[49] immortalised this inglorious episode (fig. 23). His work is as famous as that by Gaspard Duché de Vancy (1756-1788), which was created in 1786 during Lapérouse's world tour. However, while Duché de Vancy's drawing shows a certain realism, except for the indigenous women whose physique is more similar to the courtesans of Versailles than to the Pacific Islanders, Janet-Lange's engraving presents a wholly imaginary spectacle. Today, the

Fig. 23

Janet-Lange, *The expedition by the frigate La Flore to Easter Island – A detachment from the crew of La Flore toppling the Vaihu statues to bring the fragments back to France* (published on 24 August 1872 in the newspaper *L'Illustration*), work inspired by the drawings and notes of Julien Viaud (Pierre Loti). This very famous engraving is marred by obvious errors: in 1872, no Rapa Nui statue was still standing on a stone podium and the French sailors never toppled one over; they simply turned over the ones which were lying face down, to look at their faces. The name Vaihu, mentioned in the caption of this engraving, refers to a potential name for Easter Island, noted in March 1774 by George Forster, a naturalist on James Cook's second voyage around the world.

French artist would be described as a plagiarist, having been largely inspired by a Pierre Loti drawing (fig. 22). But Janet-Lange distorted Loti's imagination; in his sketch he imagined the bygone era when the *moai* were still standing. Janet-Lange took this document at face value and turned it into a seemingly realistic – albeit grandiloquent – scene that never existed: the French sailors of 1872 merely turned over a statue that was already lying face down in order to observe its face, they did not topple one that would have been standing on its pedestal in 1872. In his defence, the text by Loti was somewhat equivocal.

Fig. 24

Henri Lavachery: *The Hanga Roa Jetty* (watercolour on paper, 1934). This small jetty was built with blocks taken from Ahu o Rongo (Lavachery 1935: 64) (coll. RMAH, inv. ET.35.5.354).

Exploration of Ahu o Rongo

Ahu o Rongo would endure other destructions; notably, it was used as a quarry for the construction of a first breakwater for the small fishing port of Hanga Roa (fig. 24).[50] In 1934, Henri Lavachery discovered a site that had already been quite altered. Only a few fragments remained of the big statues that Pierre Loti had seen lying face down in 1872. On the southern side of the monument, however, this destruction had allowed the reappearance of a statue that had probably been buried under the ruins for a long time. This statue was the one that was taken to Belgium. Pou Hakanononga was not therefore lying in front or on top of the vast platform, but beside it. The small diagram drawn by Henri Lavachery in his notebook in 1934 is very clear in this regard (fig. 25), a situation confirmed by Charlie Love, Emeritus Professor of the Western Wyoming Community College in Rock Spring (Wyoming, USA), who, in 1999, created a highly detailed plan of the site.

The excavations carried out by the Royal Museums of Art and History since 2001 have therefore focused on the southern end of the site. This research was financed by the National

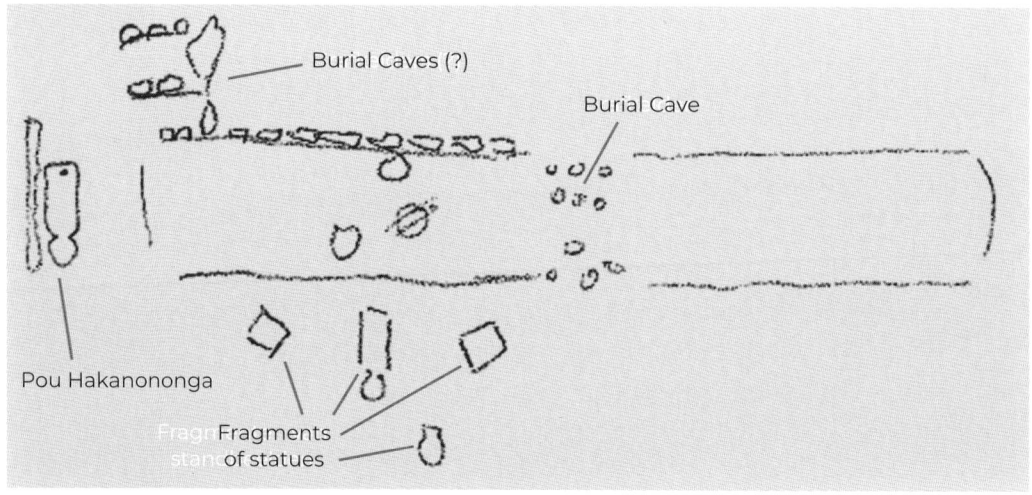

Geographic Society of Washington (USA), and since 2003 by the Belgian Federal Ministry of Science Policy (Belspo). The results of this work exceeded expectations. Indeed, it soon became apparent that Pou Hakanononga had been erected on a small platform (*ahu*), before this first monument was taken out of use and the statue was laid face down. Later, a second *ahu*, much larger, was built a little further north. Like all the statue platforms on Easter Island, this new construction consisted of a podium with a large stone terrace leading up to it on the landware side. Everywhere, these terraces or ramps (*tahua* in

Fig. 25

Henri Lavachery: *Schematic plan of Ahu o Rongo* (1934). Pou Hakanononga, the *moai* now exhibited in Brussels, stood to the south of a large statue platform (*ahu-moai*). Drawing from Henri Lavachery's notebooks.

Fig. 26

The *moai* that would be taken to Brussels, just before its removal in December 1934. The statue lies on the ruins, its face turned towards the ground

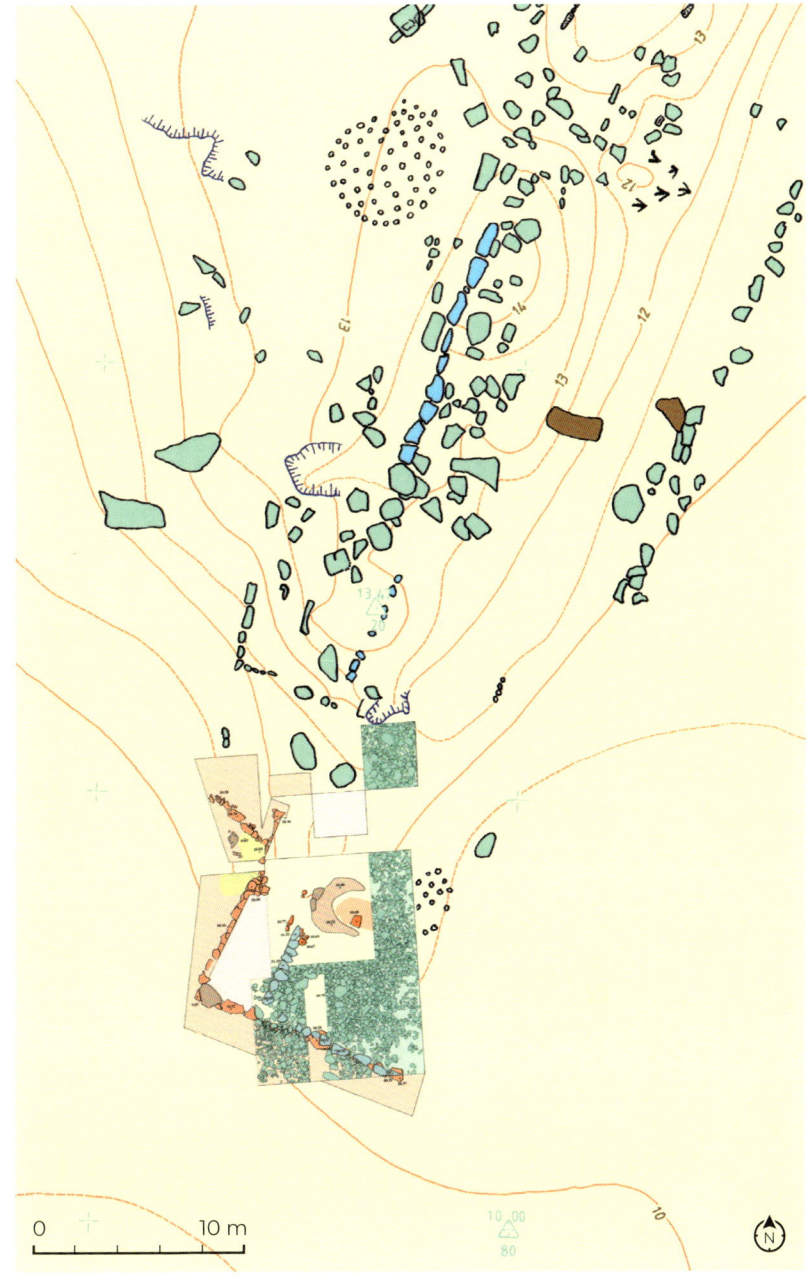

Fig. 27

Plan of the excavations carried out at Ahu o Rongo by the Royal Museums of Art and History, between 2001 and 2003. Pou Hakanononga's platform (in orange and light brown) was found under the southern wing of a more recent monument, which extends to the north (in blue and green). In dark brown are the remaining fragments of the statues of the recent *ahu*.

Polynesian) extend over a greater length than the monument they adorn. These overflow areas are often called the "wings" of the *ahu*. Ahu o Rongo's second construction was no exception, and its southern wing quite naturally covered the old altar on which Pou Hakanononga had been erected, itself buried under this new construction (fig. 26).

But modern archaeology is not satisfied with a simple description of events. They must still be placed in a chronology, which is not always easy to establish. Carbon-14 testing (^{14}C), for example, only works for organic material. However, the small monument built for Pou Hakanononga was constructed directly on a fire level. There is little doubt that this charcoal-rich layer is the remnant of the fire-clearing of the vegetation in order to build the monument. Regardless of this interpretation, by default, this burn is older, if only by a few hours, than the walls immediately above it. A sample was therefore submitted to the Centre for Isotope Research at the University of Groningen in the Netherlands, one of the oldest laboratories in the world in order to calculate ^{14}C dates. The burn under Pou Hakanononga's *ahu* appeared to have been kindled sometime between 1270 and 1400 CE. A second charcoal from the sedimentary level between the ancient *ahu* and the south wing of the more recent one was sent to the Groningen laboratory. This second sample is therefore chronologically placed between the end of use of the first monument (that of Pou Hakanononga) and the beginning of the construction of the next (the one whose statue head was sawn off by the sailors of *La Flore*). The result of this second analysis was almost identical to that of the first measurement. This means that between the end of the thirteenth century and the end of the following one, the Rapa Nui built a first platform, erected Pou Hakanononga on it, and then laid it face down on the ground, before beginning the construction of a new monument (fig. 27).[51] All these data make the Pou Hakanononga platform the oldest *ahu* currently known on the island. Undoubtedly, this is not the oldest monument on Rapa Nui, but it is the one which, in the current state of knowledge, has the earliest dating in time.

Life expectancy of the *ahu-moai*

All this may seem surprising. Were monuments made of weighty stones and supporting heavy statues really built on Easter Island, only to be dismantled a few decades later and new constructions started on which to put other *moai*? It is surprising that the Polynesians had the technical capacity to build all their statue platforms, as they had neither

Fig. 28

2007 excavations by the Royal Museums of Art and History at Ahu te Niu (northwest coast). As at Ahu o Rongo, layers of monuments were discovered on this site. Of the ancient monument, only a few elements of the cobbled ramp remain (below, in the foreground). A little further back, marked out by beautiful slabs laid on edge, the terrace of a second platform, also covered with pebbles. The *moai* associated with this second platform lies face down. This example shows how common it is, in Rapa Nui, to rebuild cult monuments, none of which were designed to stand for eternity.

wheels nor metal at their disposal. It is even more surprising that all this work was reduced to nothing at Ahu o Rongo, in order to start the task over again. We know today that this is not an exception. Wherever archaeological excavations have been carried out, the same situation has been discovered, with successions of platforms (fig. 28). This suggests that the *ahu* on Easter Island were never designed to stand the test of time and that they had a "life expectancy" of just under a century.[52]

The reasons for these cycles of construction, dismantling and reconstruction are not obvious. However, it is known that in Polynesia the aristocracy had to demonstrate their abilities, as birth alone was not always enough to ensure rank and function. Was the regular reconstruction of the cult platforms part of this requirement, allowing patrons to assert their abilities? Moreover, early evidence indicates that the Polynesians had a genealogical conception of all aspects of the world, including monuments. Thus, the large *marae* (paved ceremonial area with altars and steles) of Taputapuatea on the island of Raiatea (Society Islands, French Polynesia) is considered the ancestor of all religious constructions in Polynesia (fig. 29). Would ritualised closures and reconstructions of the *ahu-moai* be akin to the generational transmission of monuments? In the late nineteenth century, Tahitians were still able to list all the filiations involved in this or that monument, with almost every stone representing a member of a lineage.[53] But all these reconstructions were probably also in response to economic necessity. It is obvious that the construction of an *ahu-moai* required the mobilisation of a workforce, its remuneration and the organisation of its subsistence. An entire economic machine was thus set in motion: food production; the extraction of raw materials and their transportation; the shaping of the slabs for the podiums, and the sculpting of the statues… In addition, whole sections of the politico-religious structure were also activated: the lifting of taboos in order to reach such and such a resource; and the ceremonies necessary for the closing of the *ahu*, and then the opening of the subsequent ones…

The *moai* and the whale

The Pou Hakanononga monument has characteristics not commonly shared with other statue platforms. Its design is square (± 10 m on each side), rather than the usual rectangular. It also does not have "wings" like most other ahu-moai. To all appearances, the few monuments that have the same configuration, which are very rare, are more recent and seem never to have supported a single *moai* (fig. 30).

Fig. 29
Previous page:

Marae (place of worship) of Taputapuatea, island of Raiatea, Society Islands, French Polynesia. This vast complex, composed of several large, paved terraces, stone altars and steles, is considered by Polynesians, from Hawaii to New Zealand (Aotearoa in Polynesian) and Rapa Nui, as the "ancestor" of all the monuments of Polynesia.

Fig. 30   Small *ahu*, partially preserved, located inland. This small platform is reminiscent of the one on which the statue of Pou Hakanononga was erected. However, there are significant differences between the two monuments: here, the stone blocks have been very carefully bush hammered, although no *moai* seems to have been ever installed on this fragile podium.

Finally, the basalt blocks used for the construction of this platform are raw, without any trace of shaping. Chronology, size, and the nature of the masonry elements... Do all these elements refer to an archaic model? It would be dangerous to make such a claim in the absence of comparisons. For the moment, it is not possible to decide whether the Pou Hakanononga monument is an exception in terms of its role and/or function, or whether it is representative of an early phase of cult architecture. It is always hazardous to draw generalisations from single cases, the value of which can only be recognised after verification of their true uniqueness. The task is complicated because the old monuments are buried under newer ones that it would be very harmful to destroy. A Gothic church is not dismantled to verify the presence of a possible Norman foundation at a lower level!

There is one last characteristic of the Pou Hakanononga platform that is not found on the other *ahu moai* already explored by archaeologists. On the southern side of the construction, one of the basalt blocks bears engravings. Among a profusion of features that it is no longer possible to interpret today, the drawing of a cetacean can be recognised (fig. 31). The meaning of these finely cut motifs is undoubtedly irretrievably lost: are they graffiti (an unlikely solution, but why not?), elements that reinforce the monument's *mana*, the remains of a ceremony, a stone salvaged from another place, an indication of a specific function…? This non-exhaustive list is not very useful to us, in the sense that there is no argument to accredit one or other of these hypotheses.

Ceremonies around the *ahu*

Finally, near the base on which Pou Hakanononga was erected in the fourteenth century, a deposit of red dust was discovered. It is a volcanic rock, red scoria (*hanihani* in Rapanui), which was deliberately reduced to the state of dust and spread on the monument (fig. 32). This process is quite usual. Indeed, where excavations have been conducted, such deposits have regularly been uncovered (fig. 33). We are obviously in the presence of a ceremonial act, which is exceptional, because these are very often immaterial (songs, dances, prayers, services…) and there are very few archaeological examples of tangible traces associated with them. But there is more. On Easter Island, the monuments were subject to a series of gestures to end their use. In addition to the deposit of red scoria, the removal of a few pebbles that covered the wings or podiums is also frequently noticed (fig. 34). The Pou Hakanononga platform is no exception. Only a few elements of its paving were found in place, the others probably having been taken to other places (fig. 32). This phenomenon is not unique to Rapa Nui. In Tahiti, for example, the removal of a block or pebble from one altar to another ensured a family's property rights, while distributing the sacred throughout all successive monuments.[54] The removal of pebbles from the *ahu* of Rapa Nui was probably based on similar conceptions.

To all appearances, the deposit of red scoria and the removal of pebbles are part of the dynamics of the *ahu*'s regular reconstruction cycles. So, to stop using a monument was significant: it required prescribed ceremonies and gestures, as evidenced by the repetition of the same events on many statue altars. The inclusion of the Pou Hakanononga platform in these particular procedures confirms that its use was deliberately terminated, without the need to look for negative circumstances, such as outright abandonment or iconoclastic destruction. The monument was "deconsecrated" in an

Fig. 31

Engraved rock incorporated into the southern wall of the Pou Hakanononga platform.

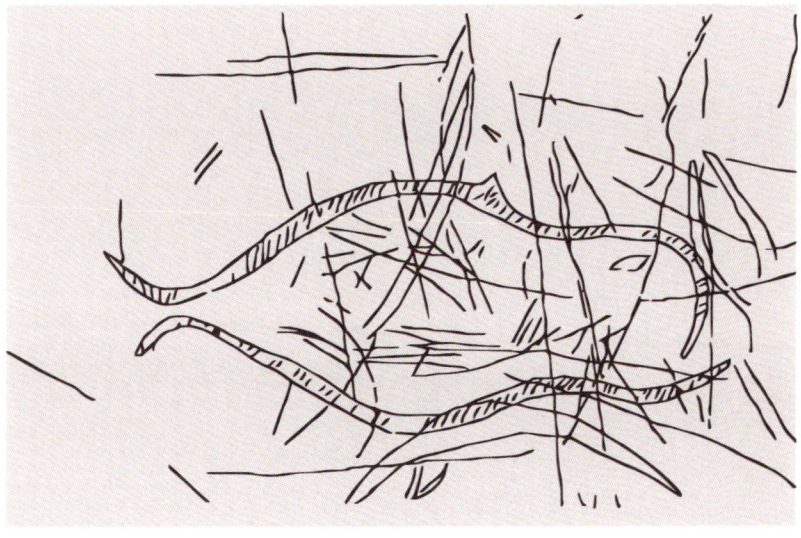

Fig. 32

Ahu o Rongo, Pou Hakanononga's ceremonial platform. The small depression in the centre of the image marks the location where Pou Hakanononga stood in the fourteenth century. Traces of red scoria dust can be seen in the foreground and on the left. There are also a few pebbles, but these would have been more numerous and would have covered the entire surface.

organised manner.

The history of the Pou Hakanononga monument is therefore fairly consistent with what is known about the more recent *ahu* on the island: its use limited in time, the closing ceremonies (red scoria and removal of pebbles), the organised depositing of the statue on the ground (without a sense of destruction), and the reconstruction of a new altar on top, which later underwent the same fate (with closing gestures and the non-violent toppling of its *moai*). All this shows that in the fourteenth century, there were already specific procedures for the dismantling and reconstruction of monuments. The only original features of the Pou

Fig. 33

Ahu Motu Toremo Hiva, Poike peninsula, far east of Rapa Nui, excavations by the Royal Museums of Art and History, 2004–2006. Almost systematically, deposits of red scoria are found on monuments at the end of their use, before new cult platforms are rebuilt on top of them.

Fig. 34

2007 excavations by the Royal Museums of Art and History at Ahu te Niu (northwest coast). On this site, as on many others, pebbles were taken from the terrace that ran up to the podium itself. If we refer to testimonies collected elsewhere in Polynesia, notably in Tahiti, these stones were undoubtedly reused in new constructions, in order to ensure the transfer of the sacred from one monument to another.

Hakanononga *ahu* are its square shape, the use of unsquared blocks for its construction, and the presence of engravings on its southern wall.

The evidence shows that the statue now on display in Brussels was hidden from view in the late fourteenth century at the latest, and that it was not visible again until the early twentieth

Fig. 35

Virtual reconstruction of the position of the Pou Hakanononga statue, as it would have been in the fourteenth century CE, standing on its altar.

century, when the more recent monument that covered it was removed. This is all it takes to confirm that its role as "god of the tuna fishermen" belongs to the resilient era of the Rapa Nui; in the distant past when it was installed on a small platform, it probably provided a more classical ministry, linked to the world of the ancestors (fig. 35).

AN ARCHAIC STATUE

Pou Hakanononga and Tukuturi

The statue of Pou Hakanononga bears little resemblance to the ones that appear in most publications about Easter Island. The first obvious difference is its general appearance: Pou Hakanononga has a round head, a poorly developed neck, and legs. Almost all other *moai* are deprived of their lower limbs and have their face separated from their body by a well-marked neck. Pou Hakanononga's legs were broken and the fragments were never found, but the tops of the thighs are vertical, which seems to indicate that the statue was possibly standing upright on its legs. However, its very prominent back of the head pulls it backwards (fig. 38). We can therefore assume that in its complete state it was on its knees, with its calves horizontal, which would prevent it from toppling over. Only one other *moai* has the same kind of configuration. This is a statue that lay buried under sediment at the foot of the southern cliff of Rano Raraku, the famous volcano that served as a

Fig. 36

Tukuturi (Kneeling), statue discovered in 1955 buried in the southeast corner of Rano Raraku, the volcano that served as a quarry for the extraction of tuff.

quarry for the extraction of tuff, from which the vast majority of the statues on Easter Island were made. This *moai* was uncovered in 1955 by the Swede Arne Skjølsvold (1925-2007), during the archaeological mission led by the Norwegian Thor Heyerdahl.[55] Once set upright, it appeared in all its originality, sitting on its heels like an orant (fig. 36). Such a configuration led the Rapanui to nickname it Tukuturi (Kneeling). Let's be honest: Pou Hakanononga and Tukuturi hardly resemble each other, except for the presence of legs and their round heads. Pou Hakanononga has straight thighs, while Tukuturi has them bent forward (fig. 37). The first is clean-shaven and has a bun, the second has a goatee (a decoration usually reserved for wooden figures) and seems to be bald (fig. 38).

There is no objective data to put Tukuturi in the time scale. Based on stylistic comparisons, Arne Skjølsvold estimated that this was an ancient *moai*. While he mentioned several

Fig. 37

Comparison of the leg position of Pou Hakanononga (right) and Tukuturi (above). Pou Hakanonong's thighs are straight, while Tukuturi's are bent forward (comparison out of scale).

Fig. 38

Comparison of the faces of Pou Hakanononga (left) and Tukuturi (above). Pou Hakanononga is clean shaven and has a bun on top of its head; Tukuturi appears bald and has a goatee (comparison out of scale).

resemblances with statues from the Marquesas and the Austral Islands (French Polynesia), he primarily highlighted the strong similarities between his *moai* and Andean statues, notably the kneeling one discovered at Tiahuanaco (Bolivia, seventh to eleventh centuries CE).[56] However, except for its position seated on the heels, there are very few elements that would ensure a relationship between the two colossi. Nevertheless, the Norwegian mission of 1955 had a very specific objective, namely to search for proof of the American origin of Polynesian societies, despite the very strong divergences between these two worlds, both linguistically and culturally, as well as in terms of economy and technical traditions. The great temples or the famous Sun Gate of Tiahuanaco, for example, have no equivalent in Polynesia. In the same way as one swallow does not make a spring, the presence of kneeling statues does not link Rapa Nui to Bolivia!

A Polynesian statue

The best comparisons for Pou Hakanononga or Tukuturi are indeed found in Polynesia (fig. 39). Here we are in the same general cultural context and the regions from which the Rapa Nui originated. Of course, the *tiki* (anthropomorphic figurations) of the Marquesas and Austral Islands are not identical to the *moai* of Easter Island. But in Polynesia, the links between the islands are proven by much archaeological evidence, notably the trade in manufactured objects.[57] At the same time, each land displays its uniqueness. Ambiguity is not part of it: while prolonged isolation can create individualisation, maintaining contacts and a global unity also forms a driver for differentiation,[58] as Nicholas Thomas reminds us: "It is difficult not to think that diversification became a goal in itself, as if the populations [of Oceania] were inventing their own artistic forms, practices and languages to define themselves and to distinguish themselves from their neighbours".[59]

The identity function is therefore strong, regardless of the intensity of the networks of contacts and trade. It is therefore time to admit that the uniqueness of Easter Island is not necessarily due to its geographical isolation. Rapa Nui belongs completely to the Polynesian universe and shares the same general cultural traits, but also the principle of a strong otherness with the other islands. It is therefore "normal" that Pou Hakanononga has a family resemblance to the statuary of the other islands, while showing originality. Staying locked in the Polynesian world to find comparisons to this *moai* is not a question of ease. It means seeing firstly how Pascuan society fits into the cultural group to which it belongs on the basis of its origins and its contacts, before looking elsewhere for similarities which are more random because they are not ensured by contexts that would explain their relevance.

In any case, Pou Hakanononga was not sculpted in accordance with the most common ideal of Rapanui statuary, but it does not yet belong to the time when the uniqueness of Easter Island had reached its peak. The *moai* of the seventeenth and eighteenth centuries are those that best assume the Rapa Nui identity. Between these and Pou Hakanononga,

Fig. 39 Examples of the statuary of the Marquesas Islands and Raivavae in the Austral Islands (French Polynesia). A–B: Lipona site, Hiva Oa island, Marquesas; C: Tikipaeke site, Nuku Hiva island, Marquesas; D: Moana Heita site, Raivavae, Austral Islands; E–F: statue known as "Smiling", Raivavae, Austral Islands; note the presence of a bun on the profile of the latter (F), as on the head of Pou Hakanononga (comparisons out of scale)

Diagram of the evolution of the Rapa Nui statuary. Pou Hakanononga (left) is the oldest *moai* currently known; it is stocky, the head is surmounted by a bun carved in the mass and it had legs which are now broken. The *moai* of Ahu Tongariki (centre) is exemplary of the golden age of platforms with statues, with no legs, hollow eyes to receive inlays, and a flat top of the head to hold a red scoria bun. The statue (on the right) of the volcano quarry, Rano Raraku, belongs to the final productions (seventeenth – eighteenth centuries); it is disproportionate (several metres high), the legless body deliberately buried in the ground, the face very elongated, the eyes marked only by deep bevels and the top of the head too narrow to take a headdress (comparison out of scale).

Fig. 40

three to four centuries of differentiation asserted the island's personality (fig. 40). Pou Hakanononga is undoubtedly the most "Polynesian" and least "Pascuan" statue. It has an undeniable archaism.

Stories of ears

Pou Hakanononga had long ears. There is nothing special about this: all the statues on Easter Island share the same distinct feature. What is surprising here is their removal (fig. 38). The regularity and perfect symmetry of the operation point to a concerted work, not an accident or a brutal destruction. The case is not entirely unique. Along the northwest coast, the modest monument at Ahu Tavake bore a statue, now lying face down, that suffered the same type of

Fig. 41

Ahu Tavake, along the northwest coast. Like Pou Hakanononga, the *moai* of this modest monument has had its ears removed.

mutilation (fig. 41). In the case of the Brussels statue, we can observe the presence of lichens in the breaks, which supports the theory that the ears were removed in the distant past. However, it is not known when the task was completed: when this *moai* was toppled over at the end of the fourteenth century, or when Pou Hakanononga reappeared, at the beginning of the twentieth, from beneath the ruins that sat on top of it?

There is a famous legend on Easter Island about short and long ears. The story goes that there was a war between two clans, the Hanau-eepe (Long Ears) and the Hanau-momoko (Short Ears). In brief, the Long Ears reduced the Short Ears to slavery, until the day when they decided to get rid of these cumbersome "commoners". But the Short Ears learned of the plan and turned the trap against their masters almost all of whom were massacred. The Short Ears took possession of the island. Much has been written about this "saga". Some have even sought out material traces of the battle,[60] which also served as the synopsis for a rather mediocre Hollywood film.[61] It is always curious to see how easily some minds take legends for facts, when these texts are used primarily to express a world view and not to record objective acts inscribed in history. After all, Heinrich Schliemann (1822-1890) did not do any better in trying to find the city of Troy, failing to perceive that Homer was first and foremost staging, in dazzling poetic form, the construction of the Greek identity. To paraphrase Jean Giraudoux (1882-1944), the Trojan War probably never happened. Neither did the one between the Hanau-eepe and Hanau-momoko!

In Rapa Nui, the only known Long Ears are the statues erected on platforms (*ahu*), those installed on the slopes of the Raraku volcano and the wooden figurines. Some supernatural beings (spirits, ghosts, ancestors...) therefore have elongated lobes. The creator deities escape this bodily modification. On the engraved rocks, the gods are often depicted without their ears, and if applicable these are drawn in "normal" proportions. Could the war referred to in the legend be a symbolic one that pitted the ancestors against the gods and which resulted in the definitive, but non-violent, dismantling of the statue platforms from the late seventeenth century and the subsequent advent of the worship of the god Makemake? Nothing can guarantee it. In any case, the existence of the legend of the Hanau-eepe and the Hanau-momoko attests to the importance of the dichotomy between long and short ears. It would therefore be tempting to imagine that the Brussels statue, once an ancestor installed on a podium, had to give up its ears to become Pou Hakanononga, the god of tuna fishermen. This free interpretation, which cannot be taken at face value, gives a better account of the cultural context of Rapa Nui than the belief in the historicity of a battle, which is told in terms of mythology.

Of flesh and bone

Pou Hakanononga's special features do not end there. Elements of its skeleton are depicted: its spine is indicated by a wide channel that flares out at the lower back; the top of its pelvic girdle is represented by a raised projection; and its collar bone is suggested by bulges between the shoulders and the neck (fig. 42). The outline of the backbone, while not very common, is not rare. Several late *moai* from Rano Raraku have their backs divided by a vertical line (fig. 43).

However, it is almost exclusively in the wooden statuary that beings are found to be "of flesh and bone". The *moai kavakava*

Fig. 42

Moai partially buried in the ground on the external slope of Rano Raraku. On the back of this statue is the indication, by a vertical line, of its spine.

Fig. 43

Statue of Pou Hakanononga, with indication of the parts of the figurative skeleton (collar bone, spine and pelvis).

– figurations (*moai*) with visible ribs (*kavakava*) – are the most typical. It is possible to see the skull (despite the presence of the flesh face), the spine, the pelvic bones and of course the rib cage (fig. 44). Supporters of the theory of the eco-suicide of the Easter Island civilisation were quick to recognise people suffering from malnutrition in these statuettes. However, it is difficult to imagine artists, trapped by rivalries between clans and fighting for their survival, developing an art of very high manufacturing quality, only to depict their contemporaries affected by deprivations worthy of the death camps of the Second World War! Here, these are instead the representation of entities that escape human nature, even if they take on its appearance, and for which all symbolic elements, whether internal or external, need to be shown. This bias, while not widespread, is found elsewhere in Polynesia, although it is best expressed on Easter Island. For example, the rib cage is regularly outlined on the small jadeite figurines from New Zealand, the *hey tiki* (fig. 45). In the Marquesas, it is not exceptional for the *tiki* to show elements of their skeleton (fig. 46). The symbolic value of the bone structure is mentioned in one of the Tahitian songs about the creation of the world: "Ta'aroa (The-unique-one) was the ancestor of all the gods;

Fig. 44

Moai kavakava ("figure with visible ribs") from Easter Island, fifteenth century (^{14}C dated) (coll. RMAH, inv. ET.48.63).

he made everything. From time immemorial was the great Ta'aroa, Tahi-tumu (The origin). Ta'aroa developed himself in solitude; he was his own parent, having no father or mother. Ta'aroa's natures were myriads: he was Ta'aroa above, Ta'aroa below, Ta'aroa in stone. Ta'aroa was a god's house; his backbone was the ridgepole, his ribs were the supporters."[62]

Fig. 45

Hey tiki (jadeite figurine) from New Zealand, where the rib cage is depicted (coll. RMAH, inv. ET.1652).

Fig. 46

Tiki from the Marquesas, Hiva Oa island, Utuka site. Under the face, in slight relief, the depiction of the collar bones ending in a hook can be seen.

The fishhooks of Pou Hakanononga

Finally, Pou Hakanononga bears a series of small, engraved motifs on its stomach and hands (fig. 47). These are circular shapes ending with a small hook. In all probability, these could be depictions of fishhooks (fig. 48), objects that were obviously common in the Polynesian islands and carried considerable allegorical weight. There is a legend about the origin of bone hooks, as recounted by Métraux: "According to an ancient myth, long ago, the natives had only stone hooks, but the fish never bit at them. Hook-fishing proved successful only after the fishermen learned from Ure-a-vai-a-nuhe [a spirit] how to make fishhooks from the bones of the dead."[63] The magical nature of fishhooks was quite appropriately used in the plot of the Disney Studios animated film *Moana*, released in 2016.

The presence of drawings of fishhooks on Pou Hakanononga's belly is therefore not insignificant. But from when do these engraved patterns date? The *moai* was found in 1935 lying on its stomach. However, it weighs nearly 6 tonnes and had probably not been turned over in recent times to have some drawings put on it. Do the engravings belong to the time when Pou Hakanononga was standing on its podium (fourteenth century)? In which case, the depiction of

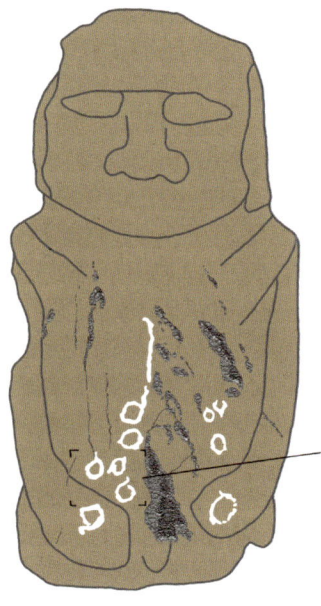

Fig. 48

Fishhooks of Rapa Nui.
A. Stone fishhook (*mangai maea*; coll. RMAH, inv. ET.35.5.118-.2).
B. Bone fishhook (*mangai ivi*; coll. RMAH, inv. ET.35.5.122).

Fig. 47

Survey of the engravings on the stomach and hands of Pou Hakanononga.

fishhooks would have no connection with the function of a fishing marker attributed to this *moai* at the beginning of the twentieth century. On the other hand, this might be linked to the engravings that decorate its *ahu*, which include the representation of a cetacean (fig. 31). This remains a hypothesis, but this fourteenth-century platform may already have had a relationship with the sea and fishing. In Tahiti, the *marae* were sometimes associated with trades, notably canoe builders or fishermen.[64] Could this have been the case in Rapa Nui?

Engravings on *moai* are quite rare. The most famous to bear some is Hoa Hakananani'a which is in the British Museum. This statue was discovered by the sailors of the HMS *Topaz*, half-buried inside a dry-stone house at the Orongo site, where the Tangata Manu (Bird Man) ceremonies, linked to the god Makemake, were held. Its back is covered entirely with motifs in relief which, in 1868, were still enhanced with a red colour that contrasted with the white paste that covered the entire body of the statue. Unfortunately, when Hoa Hakananani'a was transferred to London, the dyes were washed away by sea water and spray and disappeared forever.[65] Most of the decoration refers to the Birdman cult, which emerged quite late, probably during the seventeenth century. It therefore seems that Hoa Hakananani'a is of recent manufacture, unless it was recovered to serve as a medium for the imagery associated with Tangata Manu, which abounds at the Orongo site (fig. 49).

Fig. 49

Partial view of the engraved rocks of Mata Ngarau (Orongo site), on the ledge of Rano Kau (volcano), in the island's southwest. The theme developed here is comparable to that which decorates the back of the statue of Hoa Hakananani'a, discovered in a dry-stone house a few hundred metres away.

It is interesting to note that the two-dimensional art of Easter Island went through two phases: up to the seventeenth century, only engravings cut by stone tools were found (fig. 31), but from the time the worship of Makemake and his representative on the island (Tangata Manu) spread, artists began to use the champlevé technique, bush-hammering the rocks to leave the figurative elements in relief (fig. 49). This dichotomy is not only chronological: what is associated with the *ahu* and the *moai* is cut; what glorifies the Tangata Manu and Makemake is in relief. Pou Hakanononga and the statues of Rano Raraku bear engraved drawings, the motifs of which do not in any way allude to the Birdman. Hoa Hakananani'a is an exception, both in terms of the decorative technique

Fig. 50

Detail of the back decorating one of the semi-buried *moai* inside the Rano Raraku crater (2011 excavations by Jo Anne Van Tilburg).

(champlevé) and the themes deployed (notably the Tangata Manu). It is not a great leap to think that the London statue was indeed diverted from its primary function to become the medium, along with other rocks, for an art related to the gods. In any case, Pou Hakanononga is the oldest occurrence of engravings on a *moai*, a phenomenon that would only be discovered very late on the half-buried colossi of Rano Raraku, the backs of which bear engraved drawings that can no longer be interpreted today (fig. 50). The exception is a single *moai* (fig. 51), the left shoulder of which shows the head of the god Makemake, rightly "tattooed" in champlevé!

The "mystery" of the Rapa Nui statues

The Easter Island *moai* were and are elements that feed the fantasies of many. Since the first contacts in the eighteenth century, European sailors have talked about them in superlatives. It is useless to recall here all the abstruse theories that always flourish about them: vestiges of a lost civilisation with prodigious technologies, elements of astronomical observatories, production unequalled elsewhere in the world... and even that they're the work of extraterrestrials!

The recurring elements in all these theories are an emphasis on the large dimensions of this statuary and an affirmation of its uniqueness in the Polynesian world. In the preceding pages, we have just observed that this last point is completely unfounded. Marquesans, Tahitians, islanders from the Austral Islands and the Cook Islands... they have all produced large statues. The originality of Easter Island lies only in the scale of its production, with nearly 900 statues currently listed. As for the extravagant dimensions of the *moai* – as unquestionable "proof" of a "mystery" – these are very largely exaggerated. The only "giants" are those installed on the inner and outer slopes of the volcano quarry, Rano Raraku. There, some colossi are indeed impressive in size and several of them exceed 10 m in height. But these spectacular moai belong to a very late period (seventeenth to eighteenth centuries) and are installed where they were carved, without ever having been transported. The hundreds of *moai* that have been scattered around the island

Fig. 51

Semi-buried *moai* on the southern flank of Rano Raraku and bearing in relief the face of the god Makemake on the left shoulder.

to be erected on stone altars are more modest, with an average height of 4 m and a weight of around 6 to 8 tonnes.[66] For comparison, Michelangelo's *David* is 5.17 m high and weighs nearly 5.5 tonnes.

But the most popular theme for fantasy lovers is the "impossible" transportation of the Easter Island statues. Once again, there are many exaggerations. Most notable is the lack of criticism of the starting point. It is systematically proposed that the Rapa Nui only moved statues that had already been entirely shaped, which is a singular assumption, to say the least: transporting a rough block, which can be slid on a sleigh or a log track, is a much simpler operation than handling a colossus that has already been finished and cannot be damaged, all the more so since in Rapa Nui the vast majority of *moai* are made of tuff, a very fragile raw material. Moreover, recent excavations have revealed the presence of important layers of tuff dust in front of the altars, which indicates that the statues were finished in the very place where they were displayed. So, there is no mystery to their movement: the transportation of blocks of about ten tonnes is very common and does not require the use of sophisticated technologies. In an experiment conducted in the 1990s, Jo Anne Van Tilburg demonstrated that about seventy people working for a week were enough to move a four-tonne statue over a distance of 15 km.[67] Did you say "mystery"?

THE COUNTRY (ALMOST) WITHOUT *MOAI*

When Henri Lavachery chose a statue to take to Brussels in 1934, he was guided by technical constraints. Pou Hakanononga had three advantages for transport: it was not oversized, it lay near where the *Mercator* was moored, and it was carved from a compact rock, stronger than the tuff from which most *moai* were made. Alfred Métraux tells a very Belgian story about this: "The Commander [Remi Van de Sande], while walking on the shore, came face to face with Pou-haka-nononga, the basalt statue that we had spotted at the beginning of our stay. That evening he said: "I love this statue and I'm taking it to Belgium." His liking for it came from the fact that it was made of hard stone. There would be no disappointment with it: it was not going to break in your hands or lose its nose along the way. It was a good, solid statue with which good, solid Flemish people could get along."[68] (fig. 52).

Alfred Métraux and Henri Lavachery had no idea at that moment that they were getting their hands on one of the oldest statues on Easter Island, nor that it had so many original features. It is now known that it was erected on an altar (*ahu*) in the late thirteenth or the fourteenth century. It remained standing for only two or three generations, before being buried under the foundations of a new monument, and then reappearing among the ruins of this final building in the late nineteenth century, or even a few decades later, becoming the god of the tuna fishermen. Even in the first moments of its existence, however, it had a particular function, undoubtedly related to the ocean and the beings that populate it, as evidenced by the drawings of fishhooks

Fig. 52

Henri Lavachery (second from left) and Alfred Métraux (right), either side of Commander Remi Van de Sande on the bridge of the *Mercator* in January 1935.

that adorn its belly and the figuration of a cetacean on the southern wall of its podium.

Pou Hakanononga alone could serve to illustrate the history of Rapa Nui. Built according to Polynesian rather than Rapa Nui ideals, it bears witness to the beginnings of the great Easter Island statuary. Moreover, the removal of its ears may be related to the profound changes that affected the island in the seventeenth and eighteenth centuries, with the transition from a society under the control of its ancestors (all depicted with long ears), to a world where the creator gods (with short ears), confined until then to mythology, took things in hand. Pou Hakanononga seems to have gone through this crisis and still found some glory in joining the divine world.

The fact that this *moai* was willingly given to Belgium by the Rapa Nui in 1934 reinforces the humanism of the Franco-Belgian expedition of 1934-1935. Since then, Belgium can be proud of having maintained strong relations with Easter Island and having contributed, until very recently, to the study of its history, notably through the excavation of several monuments, which have allowed the dynamics of Rapa Nui's cult architecture to be reconstructed.[69]

Nevertheless, the question of possible restitution does arise. Appealing to the context of 1934-1935 and especially to the enthusiastic manner in which the Rapanuis accepted giving up a statue is a bit limited as a way to justify keeping Pou Hakanononga in Brussels. Returning Pou Hakanononga without further ado does not seem much more constructive. When approached by the Rapa Nui about Hoa Hakananani'a and Moai Hava – the two statues in London – the British Museum recently decided to establish a more sustained relationship with the Rapa Nui community in order to organise joint projects for the benefit of researchers, artists and all Rapanui. But the British Museum also reminds us that Hoa Hakananani'a and Moai Hava are ambassadors of a culture, especially since, in London, they benefit from a confrontation with other cultural universes with which Rapa Nui society interconnects "whether through trade, migration, conquest, peaceful exchange or other interactions, both in the past and today".[70]

Let us remember that the confinement of each society in its own past leads to a strong deterioration in the understanding of the other, which sometimes leads to intolerance of cultural differences. Conversely, depriving a community of the elements of its history is condemning it to an inability to assume its identity, a dramatic and irreversible loss. There is no easy, off-the-shelf solution. Each case requires debate and reflection, and it would be very damaging to become locked into dogmatic approaches, that of return at all costs, or of its categorical refusal. Furthermore, it would be painful

Fig. 53

Irirangi, a three-year-old Rapa Nui boy, visiting Belgium with his parents, the "country (almost) without *moai*" (July 2011).

if Pou Hakanononga had to endure the futile arguments of self-proclaimed spokespersons for minorities (now called "influencers"), whose peremptory opinions are spread at lightning speed, without them ever having to justify them. Let's hope that the mutual respect that has existed between Belgium and Rapa Nui for more than 80 years will augur well for discussions that will benefit Pascuan society and the diffusion of its history and contemporary identity.

We will end with the witty remark of Irirangi, a kid from Rapa Nui who visited Belgium with his parents about ten years ago, when he was not quite four years old (fig. 53). He wondered, with the candor of his youth, how the inhabitants of this strange country of Belgium could live without *moai*. He was reassured on seeing Pou Hakanononga in the exhibition rooms of the Art & History Museum. Phew, Belgium is not a country without *moai*!

NOTES

1. *La Libre Belgique*, 15 May 1935.
2. *Le Soir*, 15 May 1935.
3. de Hevesy 1932; *Idem* 1933.
4. Métraux 1941: 9-10.
5. Métraux 1940.
6. Lavachery 1939.
7. Lavachery 1935; Métraux 1941.
8. Barilier 2019.
9. Lavachery 2005.
10. Laurière 2014.
11. Belgian weekly magazine, no longer produced, the covers of which featured caricatures for a long time.
12. *La Nation Belge*, 29 May 1935.
13. Lavachery 1935: 257.
14. Métraux 1941: 195.
15. A copy of this letter is stored in the RMAH archives.
16. *La Libre Belgique*, 19 December 1936.
17. *Le Soir*, 15 May 1935.
18. Métraux 1941: 195.
19. Lavachery 1935: 258-259.
20. Lavachery 1935: 267-268.
21. Métraux 1941: 197.
22. Métraux 1941: 197.
23. Personal communication.
24. Beaglehole 1969: 358.
25. Métraux 1941: 143-148.
26. Routledge 1919: 183-184.
27. Englert 1978: 150.

28 https://www.britishmuseum.org (accessed 13/04/2022); Van Tilburg 2004.
29 https://www.britishmuseum.org (accessed 13/04/2022).
30 Van Tilburg 2004: 37-38.
31 Lavachery 1935: 66; Forment 1981: 134.
32 Correspondence stored in the Henri Lavachery archive at the RMAH.
33 Maria Ika in Métraux 1941: 197; Forment 1983.
34 Fischer 2005; Pinart 1878.
35 Routledge 1919: 290-302.
36 Heyerdahl 1975: 90-139.
37 Cauwe 2012.
38 John Macmillan Brown (1845-1935), a New Zealand researcher of Scottish origin who visited Easter Island in the early 1920s and for whom Juan Tepano worked as a guide, after having been Katherine Routledge's informant and before becoming informant too for the Franco-Belgian mission.
39 Lavachery 1935: 75.
40 Métraux 1941: 194-197.
41 Lavachery 1935: 257.
42 Guégan 1930: 34.
43 Métraux 1941: 23.
44 Lavachery 1935: 37-38.
45 Douglas Porteous 1981.
46 Fischer 2005.
47 The painter Thomas Couture (1815-1879), who taught Édouard Manet, became most famous for his work *The Romans in their Decadence* (1847), now kept in the Musée d'Orsay (Paris). In the lower right corner of the composition, two Romans are seen sadly contemplating their contemporaries' debauchery (https://www.musee-orsay.fr/fr/oeuvres/romains-de-la-decadence-9493; accessed on 13/04/2022).
48 Loti 1988: 43-45.
49 Bénézit 1999, vol. 7: 465.
50 Lavachery 1935: 64.
51 Huyge & Cauwe 2002.
52 Cauwe 2011.
53 Henry 1968: 148-149.
54 Henry 1968: 148-149.
55 Skjølsvold 1961: 360-362.

56 Skjølsvold 1961: 362 & pl. 53.
57 Hermann 2015; *Idem* 2016.
58 Kirch 1990; Conte 1997.
59 Thomas 1995.
60 Smith 1961.
61 *Rapa Nui* by Kevin Reynolds (1994), produced by Kevin Costner.
62 Henry 1968: 343.
63 Métraux 1940: 174 and 363.
64 Henry 1968: 155.
65 Van Tilburg 2004: 38.
66 Van Tilburg 2004: 23.
67 Van Tilburg 2004: 148-163.
68 Métraux 1941: 194.
69 Cauwe 2011.
70 https://www.britishmuseum.org/about-us/british-museum-story/contested-objects-collection/moai; accessed 02/05/2022.

REFERENCES

- —, *Hoa Hakananai'a*. https://www.britishmuseum.org/collection/object/E_Oc1869-1005-1 (accessed 28/03/2022).
- —, *Moai*. https://www.britishmuseum.org/about-us/british-museum-story/contested-objects-collection/moai (accessed 02/05/2022).
- Barilier E., 2019. *Alfred Métraux ou la Terre sans Mal.* Lausanne, Savoir Suisse, 168 pp.
- Beaglehole J.C. (ed.), 1969. *The Voyage of the Resolution and Adventure (1772-1775)*. Cambridge, University Press, 1028 pp.
- Benezit E., 1999. *Dictionnaire des peintres, sculpteurs, dessinateurs et graveurs*. Paris, Gründ (4th edition), vol. 7, 958 pp.
- Cauwe N., 2011. *Île de Pâques. Le grand tabou*. Louvain-la-Neuve, Versant Sud, 158 pp.
- Cauwe N., 2012. "Têtes coupées, têtes trophées. L'exemple de l'île de Pâques." In: Boulestin B., Henry Gambier D. (eds.), *Crânes trophées, crânes d'ancêtres et autres pratiques autour de la tête : problèmes d'interprétation en archéologie. Actes de la table ronde pluridisciplinaire, Musée national de Préhistoire, Les Eyzies-de-Tayac (Dordogne, France), 14-16 octobre 2010.* Oxford, Archaeopress (BAR International Series 2415): 21-28.
- Conte É, 1997. "La différenciation culturelle en Polynésie orientale. Propositions pour une interprétation alternative." *Journal de la Société des Océanistes*, 105: 157-171 (available on Perseus: https://www.persee.fr/doc/jso_0300-953x_1997_num_105_2_2025, accessed 19/01/2022).

- de Hevesy G., 1932. "Écriture de l'Ile de Pâques." *Bulletin de la Société des Américanistes de Belgique*, 1932: 120-127.
- de Hevesy G., 1933. "Sur une écriture océanienne paraissant d'origine néolithique." *Bulletin de la Société Préhistorique Française*, 7-8: 434-449.
- Douglas Porteous J., 1981. "The Annexation of Eastern Island: Geopolitics and Environmental Perception." *North-South Canadian Journal of Latin American Studies*, 6/11: 67-80.
- Englert S., 1978. *Idioma Rapanui. Gramatica y Diccionario del antiguo idioma de la Isla de Pascua*. Santiago, Universidad de Chile, 288 pp.
- Fischer S.R., 2005. *Island at the End of the World. The Turbulent History of Easter Island*. London, Reaktion Books, 304 pp.
- Forment F., 1981. *Le Pacifique aux îles innombrables. Île de Pâques. Catalogue d'objets de la Polynésie et de la Micronésie exposés dans la salle Mercator*. Brussels, Royal Museums of Art and History, 212 pp.
- Forment F., 1983. "Pou Hakanononga, God van de tonijnvissers?" In: *Liber Memorialis Prof. Dr. p.J. Vandenhoute 1913-1978*. Gent, Seminarie voor Etnische Kunst: 191-209.
- Guégan B., 1930. *Voyage de Lapérouse autour du Monde*. Paris, Éditions du Carrefour (from Lapérouse's handwritten notes), 294 pp.
- Henry T., 1968. *Tahiti aux temps anciens*. Paris, Société des Océanistes, 672 pp.
- Hermann A., 2015. "Dynamique de peuplement et évolution des réseaux d'échange à longue distance en Océanie." In: Naudinot N., Meignen L., Binder D. (eds.). *Les systèmes de mobilité de la Préhistoire au Moyen Âge, XXXVe Rencontres Internationales d'Archéologie et d'Histoire d'Antibes*. Antibes, Éditions APDCA: 109-125.
- Hermann A., 2016. "Production et échange des lames d'herminette en pierre en Polynésie centrale : les dynamiques techno-économiques dans l'île de Tubuai (Archipel des Australes)." In: Valentin F., Molle G. (eds.). *La pratique de l'espace en Océanie : Découverte, appropriation et émergence des systèmes sociaux traditionnels. Actes du colloque 'La pratique de l'espace en Océanie', 30/01-01/02 2014*. Paris, INHA (Séance de la Société Préhistorique Française).
- Heyerdahl T., 1975. *The Art of Easter Island*. Amsterdam, De Boekerij, 350 pp.

- Huyge D., Cauwe N., 2002. "The Ahu o Rongo Project: Archaeological Research on Rapa Nui." *Rapa Nui Journal*, 16/1: 11-16.
- Kirch P. V., 1990. "Regional variation and local style: a neglected dimension in Hawaiian Prehistory." *Pacific Studies*, 3/2: 41-24 (available at http://ojs-dev.byuh.edu/index.php/pacific/article/view/ 2760/2672; accessed 19/01/2022).
- Laurière C., 2014. *L'Odyssée pascuane. Mission Métraux-Lavachery, Île de Pâques (1934-1935)*. Paris, Les Carnets de Bérose, 200 pp.
- Lavachery H., 1935. *Île de Pâques*. Paris, Grasset, 300 pp.
- Lavachery H., 1939. *Les pétroglyphes de l'île de Pâques*. Antwerp, De Sikkel, 2 vol., 140 pp.
- Lavachery T., 2005. *Île de Pâques 1934 : deux hommes pour un mystère*. Brussels, Labor, 198 pp.
- Loti P., 1988. *L'île de Pâques. Journal d'un aspirant de "La Flore."* Ville-d'Avray, Pierre-Olivier Combelles (publication of the 1872 notebooks), 128 pp.
- Métraux A., 1940. *Ethnology of Easter Island*. Honolulu, Bernice Pauahi Bishop Museum (bulletin 160), 432 pp.
- Métraux A., 1941. *L'île de Pâques*. Paris, Gallimard, 214 pp.
- Pinart A., 1878. "Voyage à l'île de Pâques (océan Pacifique)." *Le Tour du Monde. Nouveau Journal des Voyages*, 1878/2: 225-240.
- Routledge K., 1919. *The Mystery of Easter Island*. London, Sifton, Praed & Co., 404 pp.
- Skjølsvold A., 1961. "The Stone Statues and Quarries of Rano Raraku." In: Heyerdahl T., Ferdon E.N. Jr. (eds.), *Reports of the Norwegian Archaeological Expedition to Easter Island and the East Pacific. Vol. 1: Archaeology of Easter Island*. Stockholm, Monograph of the School of American Research and the Museum of New Mexico (24/1): 339-379.
- Smith C.S., 1961. "The Poike Ditch." In: Heyerdahl T., Ferdon E.N. Jr. (eds.), *Reports of the Norwegian Archaeological Expedition to Easter Island and the East Pacific. Vol. 1: Archaeology of Easter Island*. Stockholm, Monograph of the School of American Research and the Museum of New Mexico (24/1): 385-391.
- Thomas N., 1995. *L'art de l'Océanie*. London, Thames & Hudson (L'Univers de l'Art 54), 216 pp.
- Van Tilburg J.A., 2004. *Hoa Hakananai'a*. London, British Museum Press (Objects in Focus), 64 pp.

INDEX OF POLYNESIAN TERMS USED IN THE TEXT

— **Ahu.** Ceremonial platform. Some of these have statues and are called *ahu-moai*. Ahu are the equivalent of the *marae* of the Society Islands (Tahiti, French Polynesia) or the *mea'e* of the Marquesas Islands.
— **Ahu-moai.** See "ahu".
— **Ahu o Rongo.** Current name of the monument from where the statue of Pou Hakanononga originates. This cult altar is along the west coast, inside the village of Hanga Roa.
— **Ariki.** Chief, king.
— **Hakanononga.** See "Pou Hakanononga".
— **Hanau.** Ear. According to legend, the **Hanau-eepe** (Long Ears) ruled over Easter Island and had reduced the **Hanau-momoko** (Short Ears) to slavery, before the Short Ears revolted and massacred the Long Ears.
— **Hanga.** Bay.
— **Hanga One One.** The sandy bay, a place on the west coast, near the village of Hanga Roa.
— **Hanga Roa.** Literally "Bay of Roa". Name of the modern village of Rapa Nui, on the southwest coast.
— **Hanga Roa o Tai.** Small bay near the village of Hanga Roa.
— **Hanihani.** Red-coloured volcanic scoria.
— **Hey tiki.** Anthropomorphic (*tiki*) pendant (*hey*). Jadeite pendant (green rock) from New Zealand.
— **Hoa Hakananai'a.** The "Stolen [or Forgotten] Friend", or "The Wave Tamer". Name given by the Rapa Nui in 1868 to the famous statue, the back of which is decorated with reliefs, and which has been kept in the British Museum since 1869.

- **Káhi.** Tuna.
- **Kohau rongorongo.** Talking wood. The term refers to objects (most often wooden tablets) bearing signs often interpreted as elements of writing.
- **Makemake.** The main god of Rapa Nui, whose worship resumed in the seventeenth century.
- **Mana.** Intrinsic force that occupies all things, both organic (humans, animals, plants) and things that belong to the mineral world. In Polynesia, everything has a *mana*, which is more or less powerful depending on the case or the circumstances.
- **Manutara.** Grey-backed tern (*Sterna lunata*). Migratory bird, a colony of which reaches Easter Island every spring. This bird, considered to be a messenger from the gods, was central to the Birdman ceremonies held annually at the Orongo site.
- **Marae.** Tahitian word referring to a place of worship marked by altars (*ahu*) surrounded by large, paved terraces, themselves often enclosed by low walls. Steles (standing stones) are regularly installed on both the *ahu* and the paved surfaces. In the Marquesas, this type of monument is called a *mea'e* and regularly supports statues known as *tiki*, in addition to steles.
- **Mea'e.** See *marae*.
- **Moai.** Anthropomorphic figure. The term applies to both the large stone statues and the wooden statuettes.
- **Moai Hava.** Dirty, abandoned, rejected, or lost statue. Name given by the Rapa Nui to a small statue kept in the British Museum since 1869.
- **Moai kavakava.** Wooden figure [*moai*] with visible ribs [*kavakava*]. The *moai kavakava* are one of the most important themes of the Rapa Nui statuary.
- **One.** Sand, sandy.
- **Piropiro.** Smelly. Nickname given to a statue lying on the slopes of the Raraku volcano by the Rapa Nui at the beginning of the twentieth century.
- **Poro.** Pebble.
- **Pou.** See Pou Hakanononga.
- **Pou Hakanononga.** Marker [*pou*] for a fishing area [*hakanononga*]. Name given in 1934 by the Rapa Nui to the statue that was taken to Brussels. As the Rapanui frequently use metonymy, the expression must be

understood here as the god of tuna fishermen.
- **Rano Raraku.** Rano refers to a volcano where the crater is filled by a lake. Rano Raraku is the volcano in the island's southeast that was used as a quarry for the extraction of tuff, from which the vast majority of the Easter Island statues are made.
- **Rapa Nui.** The Great Rapa, the Polynesian name for Easter Island. The inhabitants are the **Rapa Nui**, their language is **Rapanui**.
- **Rongorongo.** See *kohau rongorongo*.
- **Tahua.** Ramp or terrace (often covered with pebbles) built in front of the podiums of the cult platforms (*ahu*).
- **Tangata Manu.** Birdman. Representative on the island of the god Makemake, appointed in each spring, during a competition held on the Orongo site, on top of the Kau volcano.
- **Tapati.** Annual festival, held since 1975 in early February, to perpetuate the culture, language, and traditions of Easter Island.
- **Taputapuatea.** Cult site on the Island of Raiatea (Society Islands, Leeward Islands, French Polynesia), considered by all Polynesians, from Hawaii to New Zealand and Rapa Nui, as the ancestor of all cult monuments. This site has been a UNESCO World Heritage Site since July 2017.
- **Tiki.** Anthropomorphic figure in Eastern Polynesia (French Polynesia). The *tiki* are a kind of Polynesian Adam or ancestral dead. They are the equivalent of the large stone *moai* of Rapa Nui.
- **Tukuturi.** "The Kneeling", a name given by the Rapa Nui to the statue discovered in 1955 at Rano Raraku by the Norwegian expedition led by Thor Heyerdahl.

ILLUSTRATION CREDITS

Royal Museums of Art and History
— Cover (photo Marc-Henri Williot).
— Figs 3, 7, 16-17, 20, 24 (photos M.-H. Williot Parmentier), 27 (plan by Frans Depuydt, KULeuven), 31 (survey by Dirk Huyge), 44 (photo by Pierre Cattelain), 45 (photo by Raoul Pessemier), 47 (survey by Serge Lemaitre), 48 (photos by Marc-Henri Williot Parmentier [ET.35.5.118-.2] and Pierre Cattelain [ET.35.5.122]).

Henri Lavachery archive
— Figs 4-5, 8-10 (photos John Fernhout), 11-14 (drawing), 25-26, 52.
— pp. 14-15, 32-33, 42-43, 48-49, back cover.

Look and Learn
— Fig. 23.

Moe Varua Rapa Nui Fundación
— Fig. 19.

Author's photos
— Figs. 14 (photo), 18, 28-30, 32-39, 40-43, 46, 49-51, 53.
— pp. 110-111.

Next page:

Ahu o Rongo today, the site from which the statue of Pou Hakanononga originates

Publication
Snoeck Publishers
    Director: Philip Van Bost
    Editor: Gunther De Wit
Royal Museums of Art and History
    General Director: Géraldine David
    Publishing Manager: Alexandra De Poorter

Author
Nicolas Cauwe

Photography
Archives Henri Lavachery, Royal Museums of Art and History
Nicolas Cauwe, Curator of the Oceania Collections of the Royal Museums of Art and History
Image Studio of the Royal Museums of Art and History:
Greet Van Deuren, ADD COMMA with the help of Raoul Pessemier, Marc-Henri Williot Parmentier, Benoît Meunier and Pierre Cattelain
Survey of the petroglyphs on the statue of Pou Hakanononga:
Serge Lemaitre
Credit for other illustrations is given on page 109.

Copy-editing and proofreading
Claire Bellier, Duncan Brown

Translation into Englsh
Oneliner (www.Oneliner.be)

Graphic Design
Stef Lantsoght, Keppie & Keppie

Colour Separation
Steurs, Wijnegem

Printed in Europe

Legal deposit: D/2024/0012/20
ISBN: 9789461618825

Cover image: Detail from the face of the statue of Pou Hakanononga

The series PLUS – Masterpieces of the Royal Museums of Art and History frames important and surprising objects in a very prominent way. Scientific stories for all audiences.

Peer review
Sincere thanks to our peer reviewers Pierre Petit, Maître de recherches at FNRS and anthropologue and art historian at the Université libre de Bruxelles (ULB), and Dr. Burkhard Vogt, Honorary Director of the Kommission für Archäologie Außereuropäischer Kulturen (KAAK), at Deutsches Archäologisches Institut (DAINST), Bonn.

© Snoeck Publishers, Ghent, 2024
© Royal Museums of Art and History, Brussels, 2024
© the author and all photographers, 2024
www.snoeckpublishers.be
www.kmkg-mrah.be

All rights reserved. No part of this publication may be reproduced or transmitted in any form or by any means, electronic or mechanical, including photocopy, recording or any other information storage and retrieval system, without prior permission in writing from the publisher. Every effort has been made to contact copyright-holders of illustrations. Any copyright-holders whom we have been unable to reach or to whom inaccurate acknowledgment has been made are invited to contact the publisher.

With the support of: